Praise for
Becoming Planetary People

Poet, teacher, writer, and voice of the earth, Jim Conlon evokes profound wisdom in his new book, a tree of wisdom reflecting the rich fruits of his lifelong learning and loving the earth. His work shows a "deep catholicity," a consciousness of wholeness and wholemaking. Jim's insightful book is helpful to those seeking a deeper sense of passion and connectivity, not to the exclusion of knowledge but the inclusion of knowledge in the expansion of the heart. I highly recommend this book to those ready to love anew.

— **Ilia Delio, OSF**, Georgetown University

How education can become an action for liberation in our Planetary Age is the challenge Jim Conlon undertakes in this book. With a creative use of story, poetry, and the wisdom of the new cosmology, he pushes the encounter between science, spirituality, and eco-justice to new levels of understanding and engagement. A refreshing and challenging read.

— **Diarmuid O'Murchu MSC**

In his new book, *Becoming a Planetary People*, Jim Conlon lays out a transformative vision and process of prophetic action. At the heart of this process is a new global way of thought that integrates the Christian faith of crucifixion, resurrection, and redemption with evolutionary science and cosmology. Communities inspired by this vision are called to arise and become empowered to work to renew selves, society, and the world toward redemptive health, harmony, and peace.

— **Rosemary Radford Ruether**
Claremont Theological School and Graduate University

Visionary and educator Jim Conlon shows here the goal of personal fulfillment can be approached in combination with nurturing of faith, promotion of social justice, and working toward ecological integrity. Richly informed by recent accounts of the new cosmic story, Conlon offers a provocative synthesis of science and faith, and he does so with poetic grace.

— **John F. Haught**
Prof. Emeritus, Department of Theology
Georgetown University

The discovery that we have been constructed by an ongoing cosmic process is the greatest of the modern scientific endeavor. When Thomas Berry recognized that an epochal transition in human consciousness was underway, he became convinced that a reinterpretation of the world religions within this new evolutionary cosmology was the most significant spiritual challenge of our time. For three decades, Jim Conlon has been exploring this reinterpretation especially of Catholicism. Jim is a wonderful guide and his work is highly recommended.

—**Brian Thomas Swimme**, co-author with
Thomas Berry of *The Universe Story*

Becoming Planetary People

*Celebrations of
Earth, Art, and Spirit*

Jim Conlon

Trowbridge & Tintera Publishing
www.txt.buzz

Trowbridge & Tintera Publishing
562 Winthrop Road
Union, NJ 07083

Printed in the United States of America

Conlon, Jim, 1936-
Becoming Planetary People: Celebrations of Earth, Spirit, and Art / Jim Conlon
Print ISBN: 978-0-9964387-0-4
Ebook ISBN: 978-0-9964387-1-1

DEDICATION

To my family, friends, colleagues, and mentors—
who are themselves planetary people.

ACKNOWLEDGEMENTS

I express my gratitude to John Tintera and Trowbridge & Tintera for bringing this project to print, and to Jude Berman for her assistance with editorial development.

Contents

A Consecration 9

Foreword 11

Part I: Introduction 17

    To Ignite Our True Destiny 19

    Our Continuous Journey 23

    Historical Context 33

    Our Way Forward 41

Part II: The Five Themes 47

    On the Threshold of Beauty 49

    Our Broken Story 62

    The Challenge Now Before Us 79

    Creativity 90

    Our Vision Realized 106

Part III: Putting the Themes into Action 117

    Companions for the Way Ahead 119

    The University of the Universe 129

    Thoughts on Going Forward 140

A Consecration

The creative energy of the divine that manifests this universe
often seems distant and inaccessible.
It is like someone hiding in the shadows—
a hidden presence, always elusive.
Yet it is palpable. It is present.

Prayer is mysterious.
We may feel as if we are talking to a stranger.
We may feel as if we are being held in a soft embrace.
Yet we wonder, will there ever be an answer?
Will it be yes or no?
I often wonder during the night,
swept on by an undulating energy that tosses me to and fro
at the portals of new life.

Then I hear a silent voice whisper guidance:
Listen, listen deeply in the silence.
Someone has a word for you.

The word is this:
Trust the sacred one.
Stay open and wait.
Embrace the mystery,
the dynamics of a hidden life.
Even in your sorrow,
life will arise again
in each new moment.

Listen, listen.
Let the newness in.

Foreword

It has been almost four decades since Thomas Berry coined the phrase "the new story." To those of us who are familiar with it, there's a sense of surprise that the concept has yet to break into the mainstream. You don't hear taxi drivers or baristas talking about it. The conversation remains on the fringes of American Catholic theology, from which it emerged.

In the introduction to her book, *An Aquinas Reader,* Mary T. Clark reminds us that in the fourth century, even the bakers in cities touched by the Christian message were hotly debating Christology. What will it take to make the new story mainstream?

Part of the problem has been that the new story is too new. One of the surprising things about the Occupy movement that swept across New York City and then the world in 2011 was that the organizers went into Zuccotti Park with no formal agenda. It wasn't like so many protests in the past, where a particular injustice, such as Jim Crow or the spraying of pesticides on California fields filled with unprotected migrant workers, drew protesters into the streets. At some point *during* the Occupy sit-in, an agenda emerged: justice for "the 99 percent."

Before Zuccotti, people on Main Street were scratching their heads and asking, "What are those damn kids doing?" Afterwards, they were writing letters to the editor demanding that something be done about the "1 percent." Taxi drivers started spewing their views about the "1 percent" all over town.

In a similar way, the new story has lacked definition. Or, it has been defined by what it is not. So, what is the new story? It is founded on the idea of the *master narrative*. A master narrative is the story we tell ourselves about who we are. For most of the past 2,000 years, the master narrative of the Western world has been the story of the fall of Adam and Eve and redemption through the suffering, crucifixion, and resurrection of Jesus Christ. Thomas Berry, who was a Catholic priest, boldly confessed that this master narrative is no longer believable or even relevant to most people. He also observed that the main corollary of the story—that this life is a test run for the afterlife—has become downright dangerous due to the effects of pollution and environmental neglect. More and more people are beginning to agree with him.

Those familiar with Thomas Berry and Brian Swimme's work know the history of how we got to this point—where our old story no longer serves. It begins with the enormous paradigm shift initiated by the astronomers of the Renaissance, who proved that the sun does not rotate around the Earth. It continues through the seismic shifts initiated by Darwin and the evolutionists of the nineteenth century. And once Einstein and the quantum physicists came onto the scene, there was no going back.

If the old story is interpreted as one of fall and redemption, what then is the new story? To this point, attempts to create a new story have been largely about infusing the scientific story of our origins (i.e., the Big Bang) with the sort of heightened rhetoric that one finds in religious texts. The scientific narratives have been poeticized. The results have been quite moving. When I contemplate the new story, a scene from the incredible movie *The Right Stuff* comes to mind: as astronaut John Glenn orbits the Earth, we see Aboriginals in Australia dancing around a bonfire. The camera pans upward as embers from the fire circle up to the sky, reaching out to the tiny capsule.

And still, few people are getting out of bed in the morning inspired by the wonder and beauty of the new story. The problem lies with the Big Bang itself. It's really difficult to make the connection between it and my life. The idea of a mass of energy that existed before time and space were created is too distant and abstract. I have found that the only way I can approach the Big Bang is through the concept of the Creator God found in the scripture—or at the very least, through the "first cause" found in philosophy.

It is important to note here that nostalgia for a lost master narrative is not entirely helpful. In fact, millions of activists and good-hearted people have taken up the cause of the Earth sphere, without worrying about first fixing a broken narrative. Thankfully so. The threats of global warming, toxic waste, and species loss, and a million other heartbreaking threats to this planet Earth are too urgent.

Implicit in environmental activism is a master narrative of its own: we are given but one life, and this planet is our home. If we do not take care of her, then the air, water, and food with which she has sustained us during our lives will not be available to future generations. Those blessed people who have become vegan or climbed trees to protect the owls have required nothing but their own consciences and innate sensitivity to move into this narrative. All sensitive people participate in it to some degree.

While fixing the old narrative—or finding a new one—may seem absurd to those who are already being nurtured by the environmental movement, there are still too many people operating under the beliefs implicit in the biblical narrative. In order to rescue the Earth, we must continue the master narrative "rescue operation" begun by Berry, Swimme, and their companions. That is exactly the project of this book.

When Jim Conlon first approached me about doing a book on the implications of the new story for humanity at this time in our history, he described it as a kind of catechism. His idea was to harness this method of translating complex theological concepts into digestible chunks that could be used by generations of Catholic parents and educators. Additionally, Jim saw his project as a historical corollary to the *Summa Theologica* of St. Thomas Aquinas. In St. Thomas's day, the philosophy of Aristotle was emerging as a rival to the philosophies of Plato and Augustine, upon which church doctrine had rested for a millennium. Thomas's stroke of genius was to accept Aristotelian philosophy on its merits and incorporate it into the tradition. Ironically, Thomas's great synthesis paved the way for the scientific revolution—which is the reason we're in this muddle in the first place.

Berry, Swimme, and their successors have been at pains to avoid couching the new story in the biblical narrative. The reason, I suppose, is they felt that doing so would do violence to both. The Bible makes no mention of the Big Bang, and the Big Bang need make no mention of the Bible. With *Becoming Planetary People*, Jim Conlon is attempting to cross the beams, so to speak.

In St. Thomas's day, Aristotle was like a sticky piece of food caught in the throat of the Catholic church. Likewise the new story today. The church at first pushed back hard against modernism, which in the nineteenth century chiefly meant rational approaches to reading and interpreting the Bible, but also included political ideas, such as democracy, and scientific ones, such as Darwinism. Over the course of the last two hundred years, the church has slowly, imperceptibly stepped aside from its condemnation of most of the discoveries and innovations of modern secularism. But to step aside from is not the same as to fully embrace.

Becoming Planetary People carries forward Thomas Berry's project of infusing the scientific version of our origins with the poetry and majesty of ritualized religion. You will find in every corner of this little book rapturous psalms penned by Conlon. More importantly, the book adds to the growing chorus attempting to incorporate the beating heart of the new story into the theological body of classical Christianity. In this sense, the title of the book, "Becoming Planetary People," can be seen as an updating of the concept of "catholic"—a word that no longer automatically carries its own original meaning of "universal."

Today, a small minority of people (and that includes people of all religions and sects) believe that the evolution of humanity into a planetary people or society is inevitable. As this happens, nation states will fall away, as will instances of famine and genocide and the worst aspects of the global poverty-riches divide. We do not believe, however, that this will happen automatically. Only by working together and in concert with the Spirit of God, which we adore, will this be accomplished.

Becoming Planetary People is an important step in realizing this vision. And as Jim shows us, the renewal we long for need not leave behind the faith traditions in which we live, and from which we derive so many vital aspects. As such, the Christian and Roman Catholic motifs that the book calls upon should be taken symbolically, not literally, and be seen as one way of incorporating scientific narratives into a faith tradition.

In our longing for heaven, we Christians neglected one of the Bible's original commands: to be fruitful and shape the Earth into a just and livable planet for all. The incontrovertible facts of environmental degradation and global warming are forcing people of faith to wake up from our glorious dreams of heaven and attend to things on this earthly plane. It's important to remember that the scientific project comes with no internal stops. The implicit message of *Becoming Planetary People* is that our faith traditions—and people of faith—have a vital role to play as bearers of conscience and witnesses to a Creator God.

—John Tintera, Executive Director, Trowbridge & Tintera

PART I
Introduction

Chapter 1

To Ignite Our True Destiny

Becoming Planetary People is the result of personal re-flections and studying the work of Thomas Berry and Teilhard de Chardin and many others who have explored the integration of science, art, and mysticism and the implications for us today.

I assembled these pages with a vision hovering softly in my mind. It is a vision of hope for the emergence of a new global civilization. And it is a call to become instruments of a planetary culture that can bring healing to the world.

This vision is the natural outgrowth of my prior work. The lessons I have learned over the years are still with me today. As I review them now, I see how each has served as a stepping stone to reach the place where I now stand. May the future be populated by seekers whose sacred trust and destiny are guardians that bring vitality and beauty to the planet and its peoples.

Foremost in my mind as I ponder a global civilization are the concepts I developed that I call geo-justice and an engaged cosmology. These concepts are the main building blocks of this book.

Thomas Berry writes, "In relation to the Earth, we have been autistic for centuries." We were not able to experience the exaltation of listening to and speaking with the mountains, the rivers, the meadows, the birds, the cicadas and crickets on summer evenings. Finally, however, we have entered a new period in which this is possible.

The statesman and poet Vaclav Havel says,

"Either we have hope within us or we don't. Hope is a dimension of the soul, and it is not particularly dependent on some observation of the world…. [Hope] is not the conviction that something will turn out well, but the certainty that something makes sense regardless of how it turns out."

My hope for each of you who read these pages is that you will keep hope alive and have faith in a future that is vibrant and flourishing. May we together activate our souls, as once again we ignite our true destiny so that what is best in us and the world around us can be amplified and enhanced, and so that the culminating vision of a new global civilization will become present and possible in each of our lives.

The Quest

There is an updraft, a turbulence
that settles in the landscape of my soul.
These upstart springs,
with their problems and their promise,
inscribe a path of higher hope,
the legacy of every trodden path.
The quest of each searching heart
goes forward
to discover and activate
the verbs that animate our soul,
to tell our story
with the universe in mind.

Chapter 2

Our Continuous Journey

Thomas Berry, a Catholic priest and member of the Congregation of the Passion (CP), felt his work was to address the wider community; rarely did he frame his writing in classical theological terms. At the same time, his writings were compatible with the Catholic tradition. In one of his best known books, The Great Work, he sets forth a beautiful vision for living one's life. According to Berry, the great work is how we are able to create meaning in our lives. We can do this, he suggests, by discovering how our lives and work are related to the larger destiny of the universe itself.

Like many involved with the great work, I understand that my vision has emerged and is continually emerging from my background and experience. There is a particularity to my version of the great work that has been shaped by the circumstances of my life and the era into which I was born. By the same token, the great work of your life is unique, smelling of the Earth, weather, and fire of your life and being.

My mother's family lived in a French settlement in Canada. The French had been conquered by the British in a battle on the Plains of Abraham, and as a result, the French became a conquered people. To preserve their culture and their language, they lived together in French settlements. My mother could not speak English until she started school.

My father's family had immigrated to Canada from Ireland

to escape the famine. In many ways, they were unwelcome visitors in a new land. The mantra "No Irish need apply" named the reality that most Irish immigrants faced when they sought employment.

My French/Irish roots profoundly influenced my early years and the choices I felt called to make. I was moved to engage in justice making and to respond to the injustices that had been inflicted on my ancestors. I identified with the marginalized, and began to develop projects to help the poor, homeless, and unemployed. I wanted to provide them with the basic necessities that my French and Irish ancestors had longed for and wanted for their own lives.

Following ordination, my early years of ministry found me involved in the work of social justice. Through my parochial assignments, I became involved in programs to house the homeless, feed the hungry, and shelter the elderly and the young. I enrolled in programs to support and focus my justice work. Urban Training Centers in Toronto and Chicago, the Industrial Areas Foundation, and the Saul Alinsky Training Institute provided education in community organization and development. Study with Paulo Freire and his colleagues in the Institute for Cultural Action shined a light on his signature work, *Pedagogy of the Oppressed*, and provided me with new insights into the process of human transformation. Another influence is Msgr. Jack Egan. Jack Egan was man who loved people and loved justice, and who loved his hometown, Chicago. Margery Frisbie told his story in *An Alley in Chicago*. The title for her book came from a comment Msgr. Patrick Molloy made at a celebration, which Jack attended, of the fortieth anniversary of Molloy's ordination. During his remarks, Molloy said, "I have seen the great boulevards of the world …. But I would rather have an alley in Chicago than any one of them." When Jack heard that, he thought it a fitting descriptor for a book about his own work. Jack taught a generation of people to inform and support those working for justice. I was privileged to be one of those people. I tell more about his story and remember his lessons later in this work.

When I arrived in California in 1984, my life took a leap forward. On the West Coast, I was introduced to the work of Thomas Berry and the new story. As a result, I began to strive to make connections between what I was learning about the universe and my justice work in community organization, popular education and communication therapy, and consciousness research. This effort led to the approach I termed *geo-justice*.

Geo-Justice

On a bright summer day in 1989, I was in Costa Rica to attend a conference on Seeking the True Meaning of Peace. Many spiritual leaders, authors, and activists were present— among them the Dalai Lama and Thomas Berry. The host was Oscar Arias, president of Costa Rica and Nobel laureate for his dedication to world peace. Of all the many fine presentations made at the conference, one remains indelibly imprinted in my memory: that by Robert Muller, former United Nations assistant secretary general and chancellor of the UN University of Peace. He stood at the podium and said that we need to learn to think cosmologically and at the same time to act both globally and locally.

This simple yet profound statement was foundational for my development of geo-justice. It led me to rethink everything I had previous thought about the personal and social spheres of our existence.

After I wrote my first book, *Geo-Justice: A Preferential Option for the Earth,* in 1990, I sent a copy to Patricia Mische, co-founder of Global Education Associates. She responded by saying that the three components of geo-justice—global, local, psycho-social—corresponded to the three principles of the universe found in the writings of Teilhard de Chardin and Thomas Berry. These principles are differentiation, interiority, and communion.

I began to see that the work of geo-justice was governed by these three dynamic principles of the universe. Differentiation reveals that nothing is the same; that there is no duplication in the universe. Interiority teaches us that there is a subjectivity, a "withinness," a personality, a soul present in all of life. Communion tells us that everything in the universe is connected to everything else.

As I expanded my understanding of geo-justice, I began to explore how the work of community organizing, global education, and popular education was reflected in these three dynamic principles. The result of this reflection was as follows: Differentiation is present in the universe; the universe honors difference. In geo-justice terms, I call this the local component. Here, each person, neighborhood, and culture is respected for its intrinsic identity and purpose. Community organization is the vehicle through which we can foster diversity, justice, and equality in each particular local setting.

Interiority gives expression to the psycho-social component of geo-justice. Each person and each gathering has its own inner articulation, its mysterious interior presence and gift. By honoring this sense of presence, we honor and celebrate the soul life of each person and community. We make connections between each individual's personal life and societal experience.

Communion reminds us that the universe is a communion of subjects; that is, a communion of real people, each with infinite value in the eyes of God. As a result of this experience of communion, I proposed that the dynamic interconnectedness in the universe points to the global component of geo-justice.

I wrote about these principles in my next book, *Earth Story/Sacred Story.* The following is a graphic representation of the components of geo-justice and their relationship to the basic principles of the universe:

Universal Principle	Geo-Justice Component
Differentiation	Local/community organization
Interiority	Psych-social component, popular education and communication therapy
Communion	Global engagement, global education

As a result of my continued pondering of Robert Muller's invitation to think cosmologically, I began to think about my fascination with science and its implication for justice and Christian spirituality. I felt unexpectedly seized by a fresh, hope-filled vision; in my imagination, the membrane between the cosmos and the soul was dissolving. With new energy, I set out to create a dynamic integration between the universe and the psyche, and from that place, to contemplate questions that had hovered in my heart for many years.

Engaged Cosmology

Thomas Berry dedicated his life to alleviating the pain of the planet and its people, yet to a large degree he left it to others to put his vision into practice and transform the culture. As I pondered how best to accomplish this and to explore the connection between cosmology and justice, my mind turned to the work of the Buddhist teacher Thich Nhat Hanh. He refers to his work as *engaged Buddhism*. I concluded that in a parallel fashion, we could call our work *engaged cosmology*. In a sense, engaged cosmology is a synthesis of what I learned from Jack Egan and Robert Muller. It was born out of the felt need to connect my newfound understanding of the universe to a set of practical strategies that could bring harmony, balance, and peace back into the world.

As my reflections deepened, I also began to see how communion, differentiation, and interiority could be understood as the ways in which the Christian doctrine of the Trinity is manifest in the world around us. Communion gives expression to the Spirit God; differentiation manifests the Creator God; and interiority the Word of God, the Son. In this way, we are able to view the universe as permeated with the divine presence. Through the work of geo-justice and engaged cosmology, we translate these principles into practical applications. Harmony and beauty flood the Earth, and the divine becomes incarnate, present throughout the Earth and all its peoples.

With *Becoming Planetary People*, I am seeking to reorient the poles of religion and cosmology. What if we were to view the Paschal mystery of Jesus' incarnation, death, and resurrection leading to Pentecost as a great cosmic narrative? In this way, incarnation expands to include the sprouting of a grain of wheat in the soil, the dawn of a new day, the vitality of a child. The crucifixion becomes a cosmic event that incorporates the encroaching death of a rainforest or a species, the poverty of a people, and the devastation of the planet.

Resurrection becomes the beginning of spring, the birth of a movement, and the fresh newness of a global civilization born out of the unleashing of the collective imagination of a people called forth at this defining moment.

By the same token, we can begin to ask ourselves how we understand the Bethlehem (incarnation), Gethsemane (crucifixion), and Easter (resurrection) moments in our lives.

Engaged cosmology involves a new synthesis of the universe story, whereby the narratives found in our sacred texts and each of our personal stories are revealed in and through our actions in the world. Engaged cosmology happens when our actions flow out of the essential connection between personal, planetary, and sacred stories.

Engaged cosmology is empowered by reflecting on the full spectrum of theology. This involves a dynamic relationship between contemplative, liberation, and creation theology. For example, we explore the longing of the soul in contemplative theology, the longing of the other in liberation theology, and the longing of the Earth in creation theology—as we reflect on the experience of mystery, creativity, and compassion

Earth, Art, and Spirit

As my notion of justice continued to evolve, I began to focus on the nature of beauty. I was inspired when I heard Brian Swimme talk about beauty as another word for justice, a notion that is also expressed in the writings of Alfred North Whitehead. I asked myself, what if we were to equate the notions of justice and beauty? We know from experience that the reverse is true: injustices are by nature ugly, repellent. They fill us with anger. I saw the need for us to transform our understanding of justice making such that we were not addressing the question "What am I angry about?" but instead asking, "What do I want to create?" With this book, I hope to further shift the conversation about justice so it can embrace the need for each member of the Earth community to find his or her personal great work. When this happens, beauty will shine forth and justice will reign supreme.

To this end, I have integrated two additional components into the concept of geo-justice. The first is personal story. Each person has a story to tell, and all stories matter. Our stories remind us of pain, celebrate joy, and consecrate sorrow. We are all called to transform the pain in our lives with what will be fuel for the liberating work of justice making. The second is the embrace of each person's faith and cultural traditions. As a Christian, I reflect on these words of the prophet Isaiah:

> "He will never waiver nor be crushed
> Until true justice is established on Earth."

The combination of geo-justice, engaged cosmology, personal story, and faith is the backbone of this book. In my own life, I have arrived at a new vision of cosmic energies and the interconnectedness of everything with everything else. I now see that the new cosmology provides a vision of reality that invites us to redefine our understanding of the divine, humanity, the meaning of life, and the universe itself. No longer do I see God as a distant judge, but rather as a benevolent presence who gives expression to compassion.

It is my hope that this new perspective will evoke in you acts of justice and healing for the Earth and its peoples. Each person can now be understood as a participant in this amazing evolutionary process. I see, with Fritof Capra, a global civilization that is a living organism made of thousands upon thousands of self-organizing networks. We move forward, energized by a unifying vision, a tapestry of relationships woven into a cosmic dance of holistic relationships.

We share a common origin and are all cousins and kin. In our interconnectedness, all barriers are removed. We become one people bound together in a mystical prophetic movement of justice, compassion, and peace. With intuition and imagination, we honor beauty as our goal.

As we look to the future, we see an evolving culture and spirituality that are deeply connected to the Earth. We see the flowering of a global movement that is growing out of the transformation of human consciousness. Out of this flows a profound cultural therapy to make possible a mutually enhancing human presence on Earth.

The culminating vision of this work of justice-making is expressed in the mantra, "Another world is possible." We understand this world as "a new kind of civil society" and understand that this new society will be global in its scope and organization. Communities will be formed at the grassroots level, linked through electronic networks formed around the world. I view the future global civilization as an emergent network rather than a machine. And I look to the future with an enduring hope that the dramatic transformation of society and soul awaits us.

Celebrate

Embrace cosmos and soul.
Celebrate the power of love,
the possibility of connection.
Experience creation's beauty,
aspirations of the heart.
Explore mystery.
Engage the adventure
of an unfinished life.
Amidst the beauty and the sorrow,
a new capacity is born.
Uncover each day
greater possibility of joy, of healing.
Create a new global civilization.

Chapter 3

Historical Context

Throughout history, many prophetic voices have resounded. Worldviews have changed and evolved. As Leonardo Boff states, "Each great turn of history introduces a new paradigm. This means that new forms of perceiving and interpreting reality emerge, and that we are obliged to redefine the fundamental concepts that orient our social and personal lives, including our concepts of God, human beings, history, the meaning of existence, and the universe."

During the Middle Ages, Aristotle's worldview began to exert a profound impact on the Western world, and a shift in consciousness took place in the West. The Christian leaders of the West invited the Dominican friar Thomas Aquinas to Rome, the seat of Christianity in the pre-reformation world. His task was to examine the Christian perspective on life in the light of Aristotelian cosmology.

Aquinas undertook his task with great vigor and intellectual insight. The result was the production of many volumes of theology, now understood as the *Summa Theologica*. Those with roots in the Christian tradition will be familiar with the writings of Aquinas. Others may wish to delve into this rich piece of our history. Thomas Berry often quoted Aquinas in his talks and writing; in fact, when he joined the Passionist Community, he took the name Thomas because of his connection to Aquinas.

In the wake of Aquinas's transitional moment, members of the believing community began to develop ways to pass on their tradition, now seen through the lens of Aristotle's work. To do this, they composed themes central to their tradition.

For a long time, I have been fascinated with the writings of Aquinas because I feel he accomplished in his time what in many ways we are challenged to accomplish in ours. The challenge is to create a dynamic integration between our worldview and our Christian tradition. It is a challenge that is very much needed today, as the mundane world in which we live and the world of faith seem to be growing further and further apart.

Thomas Berry clearly articulated the relevance of his namesake's work for our world today:

> "As Thomas Aquinas gave vigor to the Christian faith through his interpretation of Aristotle, so now a new vision and a new vigor are available through our modern understanding of the origin and development of the universe and the emerging ecological age. If creating the new cultural coding is the next phase of the American experience, creating this new cultural coding may well be the next phase of the Christian tradition."

It is both our privilege and our challenge to engage in the process of imagining the Christian message filtered to us through the eyes of evolutionary science and the new cosmology. Aquinas was able to do this in the past, and the result was a revitalized Christianity. In our life time, however, we have seen a decline in interest in the Christian life because our Christian story has been overshadowed by the dominance of the consumer-driven culture. Moreover, the medieval perspective of Aquinas remains with us, dictating our philosophy and theology, as it did when I was in the seminary. We are frozen in a static dogma, which is inadequate to capture the integration of spirituality and science that is needed to reinvigorate our tradition.

Teilhard de Chardin warns in no uncertain terms, "Christianity will never cease to stagnate, will never begin once more to spread with the vigour of its early days, unless it makes up its mind to gear itself to the natural aspirations of the Earth." And Ilia Delio names the problem this way: "Christian theology no longer has an effective cosmology that enables believers to relate to the world in its physical character in a way that is consistent with religious symbols. We have yet to reframe our hopes in light of an expanding universe."

With many others, I share the challenge presented by Ilia Delio. I, too, feel deeply the decreased relevance of the Christian faith in the modern world. As a result, I want to contribute to a new integration between the Christian world—which seems somehow to have become frozen in time, and is now viewed as a medieval church in a postmodern world—and the world as we see it today, through the lens of evolutionary science.

John Grim writes, "Aquinas exemplifies an archetypal pattern of architectonic thinker in the thirteenth century who drew on the newly arrived classical thought of Aristotle to creatively synthesize the thought of his age." In Aristotelian thought, Aquinas found the means to articulate the philosophic version of the story for his time.

During the Great Depression, Peter Maurin and Dorothy Day cofounded the Catholic Worker, an organization designed to support the working poor and spread awareness of social justice. Their newspaper of the same name still sells for one penny a copy. In her autobiography, Dorothy describes

Peter's desire to make Christianity relevant for the times: "He wanted to make a new synthesis, as St. Thomas had done in the Middle Ages, and he wanted to enlist the aid of a group of people in doing this. He was no more afraid of non-Catholic approach to problems than St. Thomas was of the Aristotelian."

It is this desire that I share with many others today. I want to affirm that Christianity need not fear new worldviews or science; rather, we can interact without fear of the new ideas present in science and culture. Much as Thomas Aquinas delved into the earlier worldview of Aristotle, we are challenged to delve fearlessly into the new worldview today, as revealed by evolutionary science, and use it to invigorate the world of faith and the Christian tradition.

We are entering a new era that invites religious people to be more sensitive to those from different cultures, races, and creeds. It is time to actively embrace science, and even to apologize for the harm our religious traditions caused—directly and indirectly—when they refused the wisdom flowing from empirical observation. We look back and remember that our forbearers put Galileo in jail. We have denigrated some of the world's greatest scientists and thinkers, such as Edwin Hubble; Albert Einstein; and even Teilhard de Chardin, who was unable to publish theological writings during his lifetime.

Today, a new sense of enthusiasm is dawning in the lives of those who embrace both the wisdom of science and their spiritual tradition. For this to happen on an even broader scale, our challenge is to reimagine our inherited traditions within the narrative of contemporary science. We can now reflect on what we have learned from Galileo, Einstein, and others and see how their wisdom actually enhances the sacredness of the Earth's story. We are challenged to ponder deeply the key components of our tradition and re-envision them in the light of what science reveals to us today. Mary Evelyn Tucker states, "We now have the capacity to tell a comprehensive story, drawing on astronomy and physics to explain the emergence of galaxies and stars, geology and chemistry to understand the formation of Earth, biology and botany to trace life evolution, and anthropology and history to see the rise of humans."

We take up the challenge to foster and make shareable with new vigor a spirituality informed by modern science. We are able to articulate a fresh understanding of spirituality that flows from the insights of evolutionary science.

Nor is this a one-way street. Just as spirit moves toward science, so too must science move toward spirit. We are indeed fortunate to live in an era when these two mighty oceans are flowing into one another. As Brian Swimme states,

"Enormous technology wielded by a single species without cosmological wisdom is degrading life everywhere. But even at this nadir of human history, a remarkable reversal has begun to take place. After science has roamed about destroying the traditional cosmologies through every continent, it is now beginning to be assimilated in a new cosmological wisdom.... We have before us the possibility for a radically new orientation in the universe... a synthesis of the evolutionary universe as discovered by science with the sacred universe as understood by our spiritual traditions."

Here at the threshold of a new beginning, we feel stirred in our depths by the conviction that our vocational destiny is to bring beauty into the world, to open our hearts to the invitation to make all our lives matter, and to become people of generosity and justice. We take both science and religion as companions as we set out to bring beauty, peace, and justice more fully into the world.

Listen

Goodness is our inheritance,
wisdom is our guide,
the stars our trajectory,
sunshine our power.

Listen carefully
to all that you may hear.
Listen to the inner voice
that calls out so loud and clear.

Chapter 4

Our Way Forward

B ased on the conviction that worldviews create worlds, I suggest that the science of evolution has given us a new view of the world and that we are at a turning point in human/Earth history. Just as Christians in the Middle Ages re-envisioned civilization in light of the worldviews of their time, so we are called to give birth to new forms of life and lifestyles in our time.

The vision of a new global civilization will involve the creative transformation of the whole world into a single community, the joining together of diverse people across the planet.

As people of faith, we find ourselves at a new moment. This new time invites us to explore this new understanding of the world from a faith perspective.

Books have been written, films produced, and programs offered. Our next step is a process to engage people and help them reflect on the foundational ideas of a living cosmology.

As a result of this process, in the coming era, each of us will be awake and each of us, in effect, will become a leader. Everyone will lead, and everyone will follow, as well. Through reflection on a collection of key themes, we will work together to contribute to the emergence of a new global civilization and to make possible a world of harmony, balance, and peace.

The universe story, the great work, and creation spiritually—as articulated in the writing of Thomas Berry—are the foundational themes that underlie our vision:

The Universe Story: The emergent story of the universe, its unfolding in time, and humanity's place in this unfolding

The Great Work: The way in which we lend our energy and focus to the unfolding dynamics of the universe, and fulfill our destiny by connecting our particular gifts to the dynamic process available in the larger arc of the universe and to the needs of our time

Creation Spirituality: How we amplify our personal quest for a full and meaningful life by enhancing our relationship to the divine and to other humans, and by viewing the natural world not only as sacred but also as a source of primary revelation

These three components of Thomas's vision converge and infuse each other. The universe story awakens us to our deep belonging in the universe, while the great work animates our soul as we take that sense of belonging forward into life and align our energies with the great unfolding. Creation spirituality bathes us in a profound awareness of the sacredness of all that is, both within the universe and in our work in this world.

Building on the work of Thomas Berry, I describe five themes that lead us into the future. The focus and intent is to propose a process through which we can reflect as individuals or in groups on the key themes of Earth, art, and spirit, and in so doing, become leaders in the creation of a new global civilization.

The Five Themes

1. On the Threshold of Beauty

We begin our journey with a spirit of celebration. We start with a brief glimpse of beauty and of the new global civilization we are about to embrace. We are stirred by a passionate vision of what the world can become when all members of the Earth community evolve and express themselves in full realization. With this first theme, we appreciate the end result of the themes that follow.

2. Our Broken Story

When science overwhelmed the traditions of philosophy and theology, the sacred story of humanity was broken. With this theme, we realize the impact of this breakage on our world and our psyche. When our tradition is reduced to static dogma and our traditional story is diminished, and when science is not yet understood as a sacred story, we become lost. We are disconnected from the past and lack a sense of the future.

3. The Challenge Before Us Now

The spirituality that is most alive today is based on an integration of our inherited tradition and an evolutionary worldview. Our challenge is to infuse this emerging spirituality into every aspect of life. With this theme, we understand that this challenge can be articulated in many ways; for example, as a fresh sense of the sacred, and as what Dr. Martin Luther King, Jr. called "the fierce urgency of now." Whatever way we express it, we can say with certitude that the future is no longer open ended, postponement is not the answer, and a collective response is called for.

4. Creativity

Creativity is the nexus from which our vision for a new civilization is born. With this theme, we realize that we are called today to create a fresh and vibrant beauty that was not here before. Our challenge—which is also our gift—is to plunge courageously into deep wells of wisdom and to realize that the creative energy of the divine is bubbling up and pulsating through every molecule and person on this sacred Earth.

5. Our Vision Realized

In the culminating theme, we cross the threshold into a new planetary civilization in which beauty shines forth as our story continues to unfold in an always yet-unfinished world. Here we realize not only the goals and purposes of the global civilization, but the strategies and actions necessary to accomplish it. Through each new image, metaphor, and art work, we move forward to fulfill the planet and ourselves, to continually co-create the beauty we are called upon to ponder and pursue. As the new global civilization comes into focus, the whole world becomes a sacrament—every blossom of clover, every drop of rain, every intuitive thought, every song that tells of beauty, every blade of grass, every dandelion and spider's web, every moment of wonder and mystery, every greening impulse.

Turning Point

We are at a turning point
in human/Earth history.
It is a time when prompted
by the stirring in our souls
and the vast wonder of the universe,
we join with good companions
to imagine and make possible
a world of beauty, sacredness and depth.

Together we take up the task
to heal what is broken
and cross the threshold of beauty,
to make possible the seamless garment
of destiny and fulfillment
to which the Earth invites us.

BECOMING PLANETARY PEOPLE

Part II
The Five Themes

The First Theme

On the Threshold of Beauty

According to traditional approaches, we must admit to and be absolved of the mistakes of the past before we are entitled to a better future. We must confess before we are empowered to create anew. Here, however, we take the reverse approach. We first inspire ourselves with a glimpse of where we are headed. We let this foretaste of a new civilization guide our hearts as we move to make it a reality.

One day during a conference on race and cosmology, Brian Swimme said the work of justice creates the conditions for beauty to shine forth. His words challenged me to reexamine my experience of beauty. As I did so, the words of medieval mystic Meister Eckhart came to mind:

> "You may call God love, You may call God goodness, But the best name for God is compassion."

For many of us, memories of our encounters with the natural world during our youth have prompted us to act on behalf of creation later in life. Those encounters instilled in us an awareness that led us to action. As adults, we understand this integration of our experience of creation as a new spiritual sensitivity. For myself, it began with a huge maple tree that stood tall in the backyard of my family home. It was also the beautiful St. Clair River, which flowed downstream one short block from where I lived, carrying the sacred cargo of freshwater fish, eager swimmers, and the glistening radiance of the midday sun.

As a child—undoubtedly like you—I was able to view the beauty of the natural world and somehow know that the God of the cosmos had come home to Earth. With Elizabeth Johnson, I can now celebrate and say, "What is crucial for a viable future is a religious spirit that converts us to the earth." I envision a new global civilization that flows from this perspective.

Beauty is the culmination of our journey, our fulfilled purpose. We stand on the threshold, letting the mountains sing to us of beauty, compassion, and sacredness, knowing that our path leads to this world of wonder.

Like a stream that flows into empty channels, we move forward empowered by the ebb and flow of existence. These undulating energies give expression to a life of goodness and hope, aligned with the deepest tendencies present in the universe and in each imagination.

We activate our inner depths and embrace the wonder of the Milky Way galaxy, the soaring stature of a mountain, the greening power of a flower, and the radical amazement of a human. We long to manifest what we see, and through cosmic engagement, bring the new story personally and culturally into the world.

As we reflect on the events that brought us here and altered our view of things, we explore what it means to be human.

We describe who we are, reflect on our activities, and ponder the questions that arise from the flow of human history.

Today we are at a new moment of grace. A new perspective has cascaded into consciousness. We have begun to discover what it means to come into alignment with the evolving universe and into alignment with God.

Today we know that the universe itself is the manifestation of divinity. We have discovered that to be human is to change our consciousness to be in alignment with the radiant energy of the universe.

Out of ambiguity, new understandings emerge. From this vast search for meaning, a new depth of understanding arises, a new sense of the sacred significance of this moment. As John O'Donohue says, "The beautiful stirs passion and urgency in us.... It unites us again with the neglected and forgotten grandeur of life."

Now is the time to reinvent our human story—or as Thomas Berry says, "The historical mission of our times is to reinvent the human." Each person is called to express wonder. As we sink deeply into this wonder, we begin to see things differently.

We move into another mode of consciousness. Conflicts, alienation, and inequalities melt away, and we become engaged in making possible a mutually enhancing story for the world.

Connecting Spirituality and Science

Within our tradition, we understand the incarnation as the birth of the historical Jesus in a manger in Bethlehem some 2000 years ago. We learn from science that the incarnation began some 14 billion years ago with the original flaring forth. Now we see that the incarnation is one continuous event, evolving from the birth of the universe until today. As we reflect on the birth of galaxies and stars and the emergence of life and consciousness, we understand that the divine has been infused into everything since the very beginning. What we celebrate as Christmas is a special event in this evolutionary process; it is a defining moment when we remember that the son of God became man and lived among us.

As we go forward, we ponder, "Where is Bethlehem today?"

First we may remember our childhood experience of Christmas and the story we heard about the child in Bethlehem with Mary, Joseph, and wise men from the East. These memories bring Bethlehem into our lives. And I also believe Bethlehem is with us every time we see flowers bloom, a child born, the sun rise, or a project flourish.

Elizabeth Johnson says, "If the great, unknowable mystery of God is pictured as the glowing sun, and God incarnate as a ray of that same light streaming to the Earth... then Spirit is the point of light that actually arrives and affects the Earth with warmth and energy."

In our world today, we experience and re-experience the beauty of new life. Each incarnational moment becomes a portal to the sacred. And each moment takes us to a fresh incarnational moment, a Bethlehem moment when the God of the cosmos comes to life in our midst. We see that the divine is present in every molecule of existence and every tree, mountain, and river. In the heartbeat of every searching soul, life takes on a quest for the divine to heal our sacred world.

A Fresh Moment of Awe and Wonder

We live at a turning point in human/Earth history. Joanna Macy says, "Future generations, if there is a livable world for them, will look back at the epochal transition we are making to a life-sustaining society. And they may well call this the time of the Great Turning." We are faced with both great challenges and enormous possibility—the possibilities of goodness, fulfillment, beauty, and peace.

In years past, people tended to embrace a story that made their lives possible and that supported their dreams, yet that consecrated the inevitable sorrows of life. Nonetheless, throughout history, humanity on occasion has awakened to the promise of a new civilization.

Perhaps you, too, long for a time when you can join other companions on the journey, as together we re-imagine the dreams and aspirations that hover in our imaginations, waiting to be born.

With the fourteenth century Sufi poet Hafiz, we ask, "How did the rose ever open its heart and give to this world all its beauty?"

Perhaps you, too, share this sacred impulse to become one more companion in the unfolding mystery, to bring creativity and compassion to the world. Perhaps you, too, shiver in amazement at the awe and wonder of the universe's fresh and vibrant beauty, as it bathes every human and every other-than-human on this sacred planet we call home.

We awaken and celebrate the new story. What is being born is our new openness to beauty, which we, as people of faith, now understand to be a divine presence. As we awaken, we listen deeply with the ear of the heart. We feel prompted to give shape and form to those visionary moments that activate our imagination and provide us with contours for the cultural forms of the new world that awaits.

As you reflect on this process, ask yourself, "What would the world be like if I awoke entirely different?" You might imagine yourself as a cosmic spider weaving webs of relationships not yet experienced. Or think of yourself climbing a ladder to reach an entirely new and different world. Ask yourself what your life would be like if you took the advice of mythologist Joseph Campbell and decided not to climb any ladder that leads to a destination where you will subsequently only realize your ladder was leaning against the wrong wall.

Perhaps the most enduring question was asked by the poet Mary Oliver when she wrote, "Tell me, what is it you plan to do with your one wild and precious life?"

Understanding Spirituality

I understand spirituality as the sum and total of our relationships, experienced within the context of our vision of hope, love, and openness to what is new.

Spirituality, as expressed by Thomas Merton, is the call of the True Self.

Spirituality can be viewed as an enhanced sensitivity to the promptings of the divine. It can be viewed as a response to divine nudges and sacred impulses.

Teilhard de Chardin refers to spirituality when he writes, "I go down into my inmost self and there I find the wellspring that I dare to call my life."

The Sufi poet-saint Rumi says, "When you do things from your soul, you feel a river moving in you, a joy."

Rabbi Abraham Heschel named spirituality "radical amazement."

When we embrace life's great mystery with enthusiasm and a zest for life, we can explore the mystery of God's presence in and through our lives.

Through this spirituality, we experience the wonder of a night sky and are amazed by the earth bursting forth with new life. We experience the mystery of life in its many manifestations and open our hearts to ask where it all came from and where we are going.

When we are embraced by the mystery we call God and feel moved to acts of generosity, cooperation, and openness that can change our minds and heart, we are in touch with our spirituality.

Our Best Second Chance

As a people, we have many options at this juncture. Humanity can proceed to a growth model of more pollution, extinction spasm, and the diminishment of life in its many forms. Or we can take another way—a new option that is focused on the Earth and its peoples. To take this option, we must allow ourselves to be guided by wisdom and by infinite possibility. Many would say that this is "our best second chance."

With this in mind, now is the time for each of us to play a role, whether big or small, in determining the future of the planet and its peoples. From the shimmering wells of the human psyche and the upstart spring of a universe alive with wonder, now is the time for us to set out and participate in the new global civilization that is waiting to emerge in our midst.

Inspired by this fresh moment of awe and wonder, we feel once again inspired to bring to its fullest realization this moment of beauty, to create a new global civilization that is fully signified through a healed and healthy world.

As our awareness is amplified, we will move forward to realign the course of our lives and to create new and further possibilities for change. Accompanying this awareness will be a sensitivity that reminds us that the world of the human and the other-than-human world are one seamless garment to which we belong. We will achieve a new synthesis of gratitude and engagement.

When this happens, we are welcomed into a stirring in the culture and the cosmos—a new sense of place where everything belongs, a place where the experience of oneness and engagement in the world coalesce and coincide.

An Invitation to Have a Conversation

I sit here, silent in the autumn sun. A soft breeze floats around my countenance and dances toward the stream and trees below. Deep within and in the world around, I hear the whisper of the birds above and the rustle of the furred creatures below.

I gaze for a moment at the vast blue sky and am startled into a fresh awareness of the sacred beauty, both above and below.

Just for a moment, I imagine a circle of companions—a gathering in which to have a conversation and tell each other stories about the wonder of it all.

Suddenly and unbidden, I see circles of friends from cornfields in the Midwest, mountain tops and streams, oceanside and plains, coming to have a conversation about the wonder of it all and what it means: what it means for the planet and its people; what it means for now and for the future; what it means for the children of every species, and for justice and peace; what it means for melting our static views and structures, and for trusting our traditions and healing the opaque dimensions of society and soul.

Perhaps it is time to have a conversation about the fresh awareness that is bubbling up in our hearts and longing to be told across the land. Perhaps it is time to have a conversation about what we feel, see, understand, and touch; time to listen deeply to each other and discover what needs to be told.

As we reflect on what is living in our hearts and minds, I invite you to join in a conversation and explore what lies ahead.

Questions to Ask Yourself

How and where do you see beauty in this world?

What do you do in response to the beauty you perceive in this world?

What would the world around you be like if it were empowered and enhanced by your spirituality and tradition?

A Place of Spirituality

Spirituality is a place of self-discovery,
a place to heal society and self.

Spirituality is a place to escape from
meaninglessness,
from obsession, from the lack of an authentic life.

With spirituality, we develop a mature personal identity.
We ground ourselves.

Spirituality is a place to experience the
transparency
of the spirit as fear dissolves.

Within spirituality, we learn to keep growing
and drink deeply in the rivers of wisdom that flow in our
midst.

Spirituality moves us into action,
motivated by a spark in the soul,
enveloped by a consciousness that transcends separation
and ignites a cohesive whole.

The goal of spirituality
is to deliver each participant to be himself or
herself
and to create a milieu where others can do the same.
When we discover our true passion and purpose,
we know clearly what we have to do and how to begin.

The New Story Revealed

The new story is revealed to us
moment by moment
in images and sounds,
sunlight and darkness,
songs of birds, flow of rivers.
The story gives voice
to the universe's many voices
and becomes a chorus of all.

We encounter the universe
with a fresh sense of wonder
and a felt sense of amazement.
As participants in a great cosmic narrative,
we see a great sacrificial moment
being enacted in our midst,
as our hearts grow bigger,
our lives more radiant and beautiful.

Our way forward on the journey
will be a response
to whatever needs to be done.

Autumn

I have always loved the fall.
I was born in the fall,
when the golden and orange
shed their amazing beauty.

People travel across the land
and from other lands
to be bathed
in beauty all around

In my early years here,
friends would send autumn leaves
in packages
to share the autumn beauty.

Autumn reminds me of my journey.
You could say
I am in the autumn of my life,
a time to reflect on life's deeper meaning.

Call Me Maple

Great maple!
Standing stately in the yard,
green, orange and red
in the autumn sun.

With playful wonder,
children swing to and fro,
dancing in the sunlight and the shade.

They call me maple.
And of course I am
rooted deeply
in the dark, dark earth below.

I feel the gentle breeze
rustle through my branches,
while I reach upward
to the golden sun.

The Second Theme

Our Broken Story

The Garden of Eden story from the Book of Genesis is the master narrative of the West. Hearing it, people come to feel the primary goal of life is to get back to Eden, which is understood as the afterlife, or heaven. This view of life and of the Adam and Eve story is incompatible with evolutionary science because no two individuals can be understood as the parents of all humanity. Moreover, by shifting the focus to the afterlife, any lasting responsibility for the health and well-being of Earth and its peoples is removed.

The result of the Genesis story is that we have been programmed to get back to Eden. Life becomes a preparation for heaven, not an opportunity to participate in the unfinished work of an evolving universe.

It is my conviction that one reason for the empty churches we see today is that the way we tell the story of Christianity is broken.

A contributing factor to our broken story is the fact that our way of receiving guidance has been severely interrupted. In previous times, we received guidance from philosophy and theology; however, the new evolutionary science has rendered these disciplines no longer foundational for our tradition. Also, the new scientific story of evolution is insufficient as a sacred story.

However, a new movement is beginning that can bring healing to our broken story. Philosophers and theologians are beginning to reflect on the scientific story of evolution as it enters its wisdom phase. Simultaneously, cosmologists are increasingly proposing that the evolutionary story of science is a sacred story. Among their assertions is the conviction that consciousness was there from the original flaring forth.

Thomas Berry gave voice to the question confronting us now and also presented us with our current challenge when he spoke of the need to "create a new cultural coding for the next phase of the Christian tradition." Hearing these words has caused me to reflect on my personal experience and on the core message of my tradition. They challenge me to imagine why things are as they are and what could be done to make them different.

As a Catholic seminarian, one of the doorways to ordination was through studying the philosophy of Thomas Aquinas. I was taught theology within the context of this Thomistic philosophy, which we know as "the scholastic approach." Unfortunately, our tradition has become frozen in a world of scholastic Thomistic categories that have ceased to be understood, listened to, and responded to by the people of today.

Nonetheless, I strongly believe that the key gospel message remains as alive and vital today as it always has been. I believe that story, music, vision, and song can contribute to healing the violence, racial strife, urban spread, homelessness, and environmental refugees that are the result of our broken story.

As we observe the divisions between philosophy and theology and science being healed, we also heed these words of Thomas Berry: "I consider that our new understanding of the universe is a new revelatory experience…. It is the way in which the divine is presently revealing itself to us."

Though this new spiritual movement is but in its early stages—which we might describe as its "groping phase"—it is energized by passion, risk, and creativity. It is a personal, social, and cosmic movement. It is a liberation movement. It is a movement to free us from the industrial era and guide us into an ecological age.

Connecting Spirituality and Science

We remember and reflect on the crucifixion of Jesus, the ancient one of sacred days, wounded and sorrowful in the Garden of Gethsemane, giving up his life on the cross of Golgotha. We know that the sacrificial moments are reenacted over time and are painfully present among us today. Today, we view the crucifixion as a cosmic event. The death of the stars in the supernova explosions gave birth to the elements, which in turn gave birth to the planets and led to the emergence of life.

Our story of birth and new life is broken in so many ways today: the erosion of topsoil; the pollution of earth, air, and water; the death of imaginations; and the lost dreams of the young. The Occupy movement reminds us of the deep disparity between the few who are rich and the many who are poor, and of unemployment, endless war, and overwhelming poverty. We join with others today who view the Earth suffering, and together we realize that there is no death without resurrection. We are shaken from our slumber and see that we are among those who hold out hope for the world.

Many today live their Gethsemane moments in silent desperation as they experience and absorb the pain of our broken society. Like the suffering servant, their experience of crucifixion is both personal and communal. They experience each day the depletion of psychic energies required to transcend the cross of disconnection that permeates the planet.

We reflect on the last words Jesus spoke on the hill of Golgotha: "I thirst" and "Today you will be with me in paradise." We are reminded of the cosmic crucifixion taking place through the death of the rainforest, the extinction of species, children dying daily of hunger, and wars across the land. The loss of a species is like the tearing of a page from sacred scripture. Each loss in this broken story taking place in our midst diminishes the divine presence and challenges us to befriend the Earth.

Talking Boards and Stories: One Approach to Healing

I have a friend, David, who lives on a small farm north of Toronto. At his farm, he houses three horses, a small number of cattle, and a vegetable garden. In addition to caring for the land and the animals, he has one other important work. Each day, five men who are developmentally challenged arrive at the farm to be with David and each other. Their day and the quality of their relationships are inspired by the life and work of Jean Vanier.

Vanier was born and raised in the province of Quebec, Canada. His father was governor general of Canada, and his mother was widely recognized for her influence in church and society. Almost fifty years ago, Vanier moved to a small house in France and invited two men with developmental disabilities to live with him there. Based on the conviction that we are all wounded, some wounds more visible than others, his vision was to create a community with these men. They named the place L'Arche (the Ark).

My friend David; Fr. Bill Clark, SJ, a priest; and many others have taken up the challenge to build community between individuals with disabilities and those society considers able. Today, literally dozens of communities around the world are based on L'Arche.

One of the best known of these communities is Daybreak, in North Toronto, Canada. It was here that author and theologian Henri Nouwen wrote *Daybreak*. As a result of this bestselling book, the L'Arche communities began to flourish around Canada and beyond. The work became better known and understood.

Even though unable to speak aloud, the men at David's farm are able to communicate through talking boards. They point to letters to form words and express themselves fully. When a companion responds, the result is a conversation. When David shares with me transcriptions of the communication among them, I feel the intimacy and transparency in their expressions. In the following conversation, they voice their concerns about the uncertainty of the farm's future and how that will personally affect them.

First Man: I am sad because I heard that the farm is closing. My mom told me you are selling the farm. I think we should keep the farm because it is our place and I want to be here with you and my friends. I am a real person at the farm.

Second Man: My mother wants me to be at Daybreak ALL the time. But I am not happy about the farm closing. I need to be here to do my work and talk with my friends.

First Man: I think my friend needs to be here, too. I think we need to say that the farm is our place, too. We need to be here because it is where we can talk to our friends and be ourselves. It is important for me to be here because I have no place where I can talk in my life. I go crazy if I cannot talk to my friends. We need help to be able to have a voice in our lives because no one thinks we can think or talk or anything.

Fr. Bill, SJ, a Jesuit priest, offers his support to David and the men in the following reflection: "The men make it so clear how important the farm is to them, which of course is no surprise, but it is so moving to hear them say it so clearly and simply. I am praying that something good can come from this."

Scripture tells us that when we gather together to do good work, the divine is present and we become a community. Jesus announces this when he says, "Where two or three are gathered in my name, I am there in the midst of them."

When David first contacted me, he was interested in how our work in cosmology and the universe story could enhance and deepen his work on the farm.

We discussed the universe story as being about a place where everyone is included, no one is left behind, and each person is embraced and welcome. As we continued to examine the connections, it became clear to me that not only can the universe story evoke a healing for David and the men in the farm community, but they have many lessons for us, as well. We, too, can use talking boards to tell and listen to the new story. The talking boards we need can take the form of books, films, creative conversations, moments of meditation, or spending time communing with the natural world. In these ways, those of us who are unable to speak are given a new freedom. The freedom to tell our stories becomes a new chapter in the story of the universe.

The Quest for Justice

Each time I listen to the news or pick up a newspaper, I step back and wonder. It seems every news cycle is punctuated with violence, outrage, racial strife, evidence of climate change, international conflict, income inequality, riots and uprisings in the streets, and wars across the world. In the midst of this, I ask, what is the meaning of justice? And why is it so lacking in our world today?

Just for a moment, I recall the setting for the Sermon on the Mount. I visualize Jesus proclaiming the centerpiece of his message to the world—the Beatitudes. I bathe myself in the words of Matthew's Gospel [5:3] and I imagine Jesus sitting down the hill with his disciples as he begins to speak:

"Happy are the poor in spirit, for theirs is the kingdom of heaven.

Happy are the gentle, for they shall have the Earth for their heritage.

Happy are those who mourn, for they shall be comforted.

Happy are those who hunger and thirst for what is right, for they shall be satisfied.

Happy are the merciful, for they shall have mercy shown to them.

Happy are the pure in heart, for they shall see God

Happy are the peacemakers, for they shall become the sons and daughters of God.

Happy are those who are persecuted in the cause of right, for theirs is the kingdom of heaven.

Happy are you when people abuse you and persecute you and speak all kinds of calumny against you on my account.

Rejoice and be glad, for your reward will be great in heaven; this is how they persecuted the prophets before you."

I reflect on Jesus' words and wonder about their meaning for today's world. I remember those who have gone before and lived out the meaning of the Beatitudes, and those who proclaimed justice to the world. I think of Francis of Assisi, who embraced all creation as sacred and greeted the planets as Brother Sun and Sister Moon, each a manifestation of the divine.

As I reflect on the Sermon on the Mount and its meaning for justice today, I speak the following prayer, which I wrote in my book *Geo-Justice:*

Where there are ruptures in creation,
we are aroused to peace.
Where there is disquiet,
we are invited to balance.
Where there is discord,
we are attuned to resonance.
In and through the pain of our wounded
planet, we are called to make our Easter with the Earth.

Turning again to our modern world, I visualize a pilgrimage I made with Vietnamese peace activist and prophet Thich Nhat Hanh to the Vietnam Memorial in Washington DC. I recall joining the United Farm Workers on the streets of Toronto, Canada, as we demonstrated on behalf of those who harvest our food for safety in their work and justice in their wages. I remember journeying to the Bowery in New York City to visit and pay tribute to Dorothy Day, Tom Cornell, and all those in the Catholic worker movement. Dorothy, who told her story in *The Long Loneliness,* reminded us that we can see in the face of a single displaced person the face of Christ. She challenged us to treat the homeless and those rendered refugees by war with dignity and respect. As I bring to mind Dorothy's radical acceptance, I strive each day to see the countenance of Christ present in our midst.

As I join with colleagues and friends to provide beds for the homeless, food for the hungry, and work for the unemployed, I see the imprint of divinity. A prayer I wrote inspired by the words attributed to St. Francis of Assisi appeared in *From the Stars to the Street*:

> Let me be an instrument of engagement.
> Where there is turmoil,
> grant me clarity.
> Where there are structures of oppression,
> grant me the ability to act.
> Grant that I may be able to transform
> upset into moral outrage,
> systemic oppression into struggles for change, hopelessness into celebration.

As I ponder social injustice, I wonder what the world would be like if the attitude of this prayer became the mantra and measure of every person and every community.

As my reflection on justice continues, the news cycle boils over with the latest bad news. A white policeman shot a young black man in Ferguson, Missouri, and following months of deliberation, emerged free of any indictment. In Ferguson, as well as in many cities across the land, including in the San

Francisco Bay Area, the wounds caused by racism, gun violence, and racial profiling once again become open sores. The people become painfully aware that justice, equality and peace in America are promises not yet fulfilled.

We are challenged to overcome fear and realize that justice has a systemic and ecological face. We pay attention to the lessons of the poets and the prophets of yesterday and today. We wake to the realization that our endangered planet, with its beauty and its pain, is now understood as the body of God.

We understand anew that the hole in the ozone layer, the melting of ice caps, and the death of dolphins and rain forests are manifestations of the suffering present in our midst.

We experience the burning bush of divine presence palpable in our midst as a call to justice that names our proclamations to heal our wounded Earth.

We embrace the emergence of a fresh awareness of beauty unfolding in our lives. It is a fresh awareness that energizes us to widen our circle of compassion as we take up the challenge to bring beauty and justice to the world.

We move forward to make possible the beloved community envisioned by Dr. Martin Luther King, Jr.; the rules for radicals envisioned by Saul David Alinsky; and the conviction that organization is the first act of justice making, as expressed by Msgr. Jack Egan. We listen deeply to the prophetic words adapted from the writings of Johann Metz: "You can't do it justice with your back to the poor and the poor Earth." With Gustavo Gutierrez, we proclaim creation as the first act of liberation. With Meister Eckhart and Brother David Steindl-Rast, we announce that gratitude is the heart of prayer. With Thomas Berry, we embrace the conviction that the Earth itself is God's dream, and we are invited to make our contribution to the dream of the Earth.

To Heal Our Broken Story

In each human heart there is a restlessness—a feeling of being somewhat lost, unfulfilled, incomplete. Poet Adrienne Rich has said, "My heart is moved by all I cannot save: so much has been destroyed." Our response to this sense of lack of fulfillment provides the context and arena wherein life happens and the promise of peace and fulfillment resides.

Have you ever felt, for example, the impact of a broken relationship? Have you experienced the end of a friendship or seen a dream you thought would last forever subside? Perhaps it was the ending of a romantic relationship, or an unexpected diagnosis that brought you and a loved one the promise of lengthy suffering and even death.

Stephen Jenkinson in his film *Grief Walker* reflects on a conversation with someone who lives out her final days while embracing the mystery that death holds for all of us. Through workshops, lectures, and writing, and his website www.orphanwisdom.com, Stephen challenges us to transform the terror that death holds for many today. He proposes that the best way to dissolve the fear of death is to fall in love with life and to see death not as a punishment, but rather as an integral component of a great evolutionary process. In this way, he challenges us to transform and heal the brokenness that many of us have as we live out our story around end-of-life issues.

To fully heal our broken story will require us to reexamine the stories that have guided humanity to this point, yet that now seem inadequate. In the Western world, this could be said to encompass the entire story of religion and culture. We also need to heal the effects of the many years during which science was absented and outlawed from our inherited traditions. Distancing ourselves from the generations of religious people who exiled Galileo, Copernicus, and Keppler—and more recently Teilhard de Chardin—we have come to understand science as a sacred source.

As we move to heal our broken story, we need to let ourselves be guided by the genetic coding that attunes us to a world of harmony and peace. Humans possess self-reflexive consciousness and thus have a choice to make in regard to how they respond to the promptings of genetic coding and programming. To realize our dream will require us to listen deeply, both to the needs of our time and to the wordless wisdom of the divine that speaks to us from the depths of our psyche. Through this integration of society's need and our response to the divine voice that summons us to act, we can move forward at this defining moment.

This is our call and the signpost of our vocational destiny. Each idea, image, and impulse—when properly listened to and tended to—will flourish and bloom in the sunshine of our awakening awareness. It will blossom forth into the rich fulfillment of those as-yet-unwritten chapters in our as-yet-unlived lives.

Through prayer, contemplation of possibilities, and a variety of creative arts and acts, we come to trust more deeply our spiritual impulses. We are convinced that these impulses are true to our nature, and that when properly understood and supported, they will guide us into a life and planetary community predicated on goodness, wisdom, and truth. With an incarnational theology that affirms that humanity is born into goodness and is not depraved, we understand a world whose trajectory and focus are founded on a "metaphysics of goodness."

Questions to Ask Yourself

How in your experience does the state of the world fall short?

What contradiction do you see between the current state of the world and the vision you hope to realize?

What does your spiritual tradition teach you about how to respond to the brokenness awash in our world?

If I Never Become

Time races by,
leaving each new morning
positioned at the waiting room of life.
Expectations fly by.
With every new tomorrow I dare to ask,
Will there be enough tomorrows
to complete the work,
accomplish what I am here to do?
Again I ask.

Gather the Fragments

Ships drift out to sea,
airplanes launch into the sky,
divers plunge into the depths.
There is movement everywhere.

A movement is needed today
that is a fresh cosmic glue,
a sacred magnetic force
that can gather the fragments,
bring together Earth, art, and spirit
to make the world one.

Sensitivity

Feel the pain, O sacred one,
my pain, the pain of the Earth.

See the red fox trembling on the campus lawn,
searching for her home.

Look up in the sky,
beyond the leaves, tree tops and clouds.

Above and beyond the wordless sky,
I hear your voice come through.

Here, from heaven above
and earth below

Embrace again the sacred one among us now,
who utters sounds of peace.

Call to Justice

We gather as a people
called forth by trust, promise, and compassion.
We remember and give thanks
to the originating energy of the universe,
to the ancient One of ancient days,
whose vast generosity calls us forth today.

We gather in circles of compassion
and make proclamations of trust.
We celebrate and embrace our cousins of creation,
who swim in the oceans,
dance in the meadows,
and soar above us in the sky.

Mindful of the brokenness and beauty all around,
we now gather to make our Earth an altar
and give thanks for all that was and is to be.
From our planetary altar,
we behold the cosmos and the world
alive with divine energy, transfigured and transformed.

With gratitude we venture forth
to create a new heaven and a new Earth.
We are convinced the meaning and practice of justice
are unfolding in our midst.
We visualize waves of cleansing energy
bringing harmony, balance, and peace to the world and its
people.

We celebrate the rebirth of justice and peace.

The Third Theme

The Challenge Now Before Us

The challenge before us is to build bridges between the old and the new. Like Thomas Aquinas in the Middle Ages, we face the challenge of bringing the ideas of a new age of science and culture to bear on the lasting truths of our Christian faith.

The worldview of Aquinas has become less and less accessible and alive to people of faith today; there seems to be a decline in religious practice and spiritual awareness. Our challenge is to experience the eternal truths that existed in the early ages of religion.

The questions we are confronted with today are: How do we understand the God of scriptures and tradition in light of our awareness of an evolutionary, unfinished universe? What are the revelatory moments available to us when we view the world through evolutionary eyes?

Our challenge is to see that the God of the universe has come home to us in our time. That is our prayer and our spiritual practice.

The challenge before us is to trust in the divine creative energy. We experience that energy weave the fabric of creation into a tapestry of belonging, a quilt of compassion and beauty.

As we roll back the cloud of unknowing, with the soft focus of the mystic, we see the Earth before us with new eyes. We peer into the surging current of divine energy. We encounter the universe with a fresh sense of wonder and amazement. Through cosmological ears, we listen to the voices of the Earth—the rustle of the breeze, the gurgle of the brook, and the exuberance of a child. With deep wisdom, we revitalize our trust and become increasingly alert as the universe speaks words of wisdom, both mystical and prophetic, to be heard across the land.

We understand spirituality and trust as that which animates our souls and expresses itself within the human and other-than-human contexts of our lives.

We give birth to images and aspirations that are waiting to be born. As if carried by a stream that flows forward to unknown banks and empty channels, we move into the future. We follow the ebb and flow of existence and the currents of energy that find expression in the rivers of our life. We direct creative energy to the great issues of our time: a healthy planet; an exhilarant child; and the greening power of the planet across fields, rivers, forests, and mountains.

Through metaphor, image, and art, we fashion the life and purpose we are called to fulfill. Our heart grows larger and our imaginations soar. We become vibrant and alive. Existence becomes a sacrament. Every blossom, clover, drop of rain, intuitive thought; every blade of grass, song that tells of beauty, spider's web; every interlude of love, pleasure, or restraint— each is an embodiment of divinity.

We envision and anticipate the restoration of the Earth and restructuring of society. We visualize urban dwellers around the world who gather to listen and heal. They encourage programs of good work, clean water, fresh air, and safe homes for the elders and the young. They embrace life's great mystery and envision a new global civilization emerging in their midst.

To ingest all of this as our story, with Earth in mind, is our emergent spirituality.

Connecting Spirituality and Science

Even as a child, Jesus took up the challenge to fulfill his destiny and purpose. He taught in the temple when he was separated from his parents. He told them he had been to the temple because he must be about his Father's business. Later, he taught his followers many lessons in parables about love, wisdom, and compassion. He spoke of the Father's compassion, told stories about the "lilies of the field," and fed the hungry with "loaves and fishes." He "changed water into wine" at Cana, and in many other ways, brought peace, compassion, and love to the world.

As we engage in conversations with our colleagues and friends about the wonder of life and the amazing beauty present in every flower, child, river, and mountain, we ask how to understand the evolutionary story of the universe as a sacred story. We see it as a revelatory narrative that heals loneliness and alienation; reinvigorates the spirit; and provides psychic energy necessary to feed the hungry, house the homeless, and empower the poor.

Our challenge is to have a dream that is all embracing. Carl Jung reminds us that "the dream drives the action." Robert Browning proposes that a dream must exceed its grasp, or what else is heaven for? Thomas Berry tells us that a quest to heal the open wound of longing for more resides within every human heart. Our deepest desire is to heal our wounded world and our wounded hearts.

Reinventing What It Means to Be Human

Our challenge, call, and possibility are to re-imagine a better world for our children—a world without war, without imperialistic thought, and free of the aggressive and unbalanced use of the Earth's resources. We are challenged to think globally, as one tribe.

Our challenge is to embrace an artful life, whose focus is on creativity and imagination. Through creativity and the many manifestations of artful living, we will be able to reinvent not only what it means to be human, but the ways in which we lead our personal and collective lives.

Often, when nothing fresh seems to happen and new ideas are not arising, we are actually in an incubation period. To live creatively in this context requires that we embrace paradox. Sometimes what appears as an empty page can turn out to be the very landscape upon which what is unprecedented and new is revealed. It is a time when we intentionally join our energy to the divine creative energy that courses through our lives and into both our psyches and the world around us.

When this occurs, our experience of destiny is touched and we begin to engage unself-consciously in the world. We take up our great work.

Our challenge is to create an ongoing conversation between modern science and our traditional ancient wisdom. To heal the roots of our tradition, we need to transform the very impulse of the story of the Garden of Eden.

There will always be some discrepancy between the world as it is and the world as we would like it to be. Nevertheless, we continue our practices to keep us in alignment with our true self and with the imaginative impulses that guide our lives and inspire us. We do this through dialogue, reflection, and openness to the rivers of imagination as they flow into our awareness.

We know from personal experience that when our creativity does not flow, we tend to become irritable, out of sorts, or cranky. Somehow we know within our psychic depths that we are coded for creativity, and when we are not able to be creative, we experience the blocked energy.

The state of contemporary culture is such that, as a result of our cultural pathology, we have witnessed the birth of a "Prozac nation." I suggest it would be to our advantage to trade the usual forms of medication for paint, cameras, guitars, hiking boots, as well as poetry circles, prayer groups, and meditation gatherings. The planetary society will embrace all phases of life and people of all temperaments, callings, and gifts.

In the late 1970s, Thomas Berry asserted the need for a new story. He also called for the ethical sensitivity to keep our imagination vital and alive as well as for the desire and capacity to respond to the needs of our time. This means not only an awareness of our psychic depth and vitality but also a sensitivity and commitment to transformation by focusing our creative energy in and through the great opportunities of our time: a healthy planet; a spontaneous child; pure air; or a celebration of the greening power of the planet across the fields, rivers, and mountains.

Tomorrow's Challenge

The word *challenge* reminds me of many things. Games on television move toward completion as they enter the "challenge" round. In athletics, the role of the challenger has great meaning. In football and baseball, for example, teams take up the challenge to win the Super Bowl or the World Series. Prize fighters become challengers when they strive to dethrone the champion.

In popular culture, to challenge can mean to strive to displace a leader or an acknowledged champion, or to become the best at one's profession.

The spiritual challenge that life presents is expressed in the words of scientist Albert Einstein: "Our task must be to free ourselves from this prison by widening our circle of compassion to embrace all living creatures and the whole of nature and its beauty."

The challenges facing humanity in the early years of the twenty-first century were marked by the occupy movement and the Arab Spring. What the world and we as individuals need now is an antidote to greed—a new vision of enoughness with which to create a world of peace with the planet and the peoples of the planet.

Today, the entire planet needs its Arab Spring. We need to draw on creation's capacity to rise up with great generosity to meet the challenges of our day: to strengthen our hope for the future, and to make peace with the Earth and among nations. It will be a future that is alive and vibrant, energized by a shared vision of an interconnected whole. Our challenge is to actualize the vision of a future built on abundant life, joy, creativity, and right livelihood.

Our challenge for tomorrow is expressed well by Thomas Aquinas when he proclaims that God is able to create all things except God Himself or Herself. Therefore, the challenge before us is to achieve the closest approximation to the divine in this world by creating a community whose diverse expression of beauty and relationship manifests the fullest experience of the divine.

The spiritual journey culminates in a full and final realization. Among the Christian community, many understand this culminating act as the planetary Pentecost, reign of God, and the coming of the Kingdom. This latter has been more aptly reframed by Rosemary Ruether and others as "kindom."

This culminating act on the journey takes place when the historical Jesus, risen following his crucifixion, becomes alive and mystically present in each of us. We now understand this as the cosmic Christ.

The result is an enveloping divine presence that weaves together a communion of companions, united with everyone and everything. When we experience this divine creative energy alive in us, all separation dissolves. We sense a fresh relatedness and feel bathed in the mystery we call God.

As participants in this ever-expanding community of companions, we become energized to move forward to feed the hungry, house the homeless, befriend the lonely, heal what is broken, and renew the face of the Earth. A most important aspect of becoming a planetary people is the emergence of an awareness that the Earth is alive and filled with what Gerard Manley Hopkins termed the "grandeur of God." In and through our spiritual journey, we make possible the full realization of our fondest hopes and dreams.

Questions to Ask Yourself

What do you see as the greatest challenge currently facing humanity?

What can you do today to realize your dream for a better world?

Thomas Berry wrote extensively about the great work of our time; how do you understand your great work at this time in human/Earth history?

Gathering on the St. Clair

Here I am again,
at Cundick Park
on St. Clair's river shore.

To the west
I see the channel bank,
freighters sailing up and down,
welcoming fish, swimmers, boats and me.

All share the water
on this crystal sunshine
summer day.

I look at the tables,
decorated with food and drink,
at the children
eager for each delicious bite.

As the sun begins to set,
we drive off
to our place of rest.

Grateful once again
for our gathering in the garden,
here upon the St. Clair shore.

A Global People

I feel a rising today
at this Easter moment,
a new vision for the world
emerging in our midst.

May all the people
gathered by the Cosmic One
become a global people,
alive, awake and hopeful,
joyfully present everywhere.

I Want to Tell You

I want to tell you
about a way
life could be.

Gaze at the stars.
Read the scriptures of your heart.
Ascend to the larger arc of existence,
where justice reigns.
Descend to that deep and restless place,
where as-yet-unseen possibilities reside.

In this newly fashioned
place of struggle,
freedom and fulfillment await.

"Let revolution happen!"
I hear my people cry.
Heal the wound.
Bind up brokenness.
Dispel all illusions
in the secret places where they lie.

The new creation to which we aspire
is no longer a daydream,
a nightmare or
a rude awakening.

Now is the time, my friend,
to tremble, articulate and rejoice.
A life-giving, functioning world
is within our grasp.
"Yes we can" echoes once again
as we take on this new moment
and become who we were meant to be.

The Fourth Theme

Creativity

My Aunt Margaret had a well in her backyard. She called the water of her well "rock water" because it came from the rocks below the surface.

To draw water from the well, it was necessary to pour water into the pump to get it started. After the pump was primed, the water would flow.

The creative process is like my Aunt Margaret's pump. When we prime the pump, creativity will flow.

Creativity happens when we create the right conditions. It doesn't result simply from a prior plan; rather, it emerges from the imagination in a moment of spontaneity and surprise. For example, when asked about a dance she had just performed, Martha Graham replied that she could not have described her dance in advance. If she had tried to describe it in advance, it would not have been creative. To be authentically creative, it had to be born in the moment.

Theology calls this element of surprise "resurrection."

Throughout history, women and men of great hope and enduring vision have continuously raised the anticipation of people. They have envisioned a better world for children of every species. Through poetry, story, and song they imagined a future that, in the words of Teilhard de Chardin, "will be better than all the pasts." They became resurrection people focused on the fullest realization of a healed and healthy world.

We, too, can become resurrection people.

When we bring something into existence that did not previously exist, we are not only creative, but we have arrived at that place where the divine and human meet. Thus, differentiation—whereby everything is unique—can be seen as the creative art form of the divine.

Storytelling—in all its forms, but especially personal storytelling—is a creative act that involves the practices of deep listening and recognition. We know people best when they tell us their stories, and we know ourselves best when we reflect on our own story. Stories tell us who we are and what we believe. Personal stories become revelatory when we recount stories of our tradition and also reflect on the story of the universe.

Through personal storytelling, we can transform our dreams into reality. Stories shape our consciousness and alter the landscape of our souls. Our stories are personal, religious, and cosmic, and our transformation occurs on each level. Joseph Campbell says, "We must be willing to get rid of the life we planned so we can have the life that is waiting for us."

Here we celebrate the work of creativity. The nature of the divine is to be creative; we are never more ourselves than when we engage in acts of creativity. To engage in acts of creativity is to continue the work of the cosmos and create a new civilization.

Connecting Spirituality and Science

Easter is a glorious time when we ponder the mystery of the empty tomb of Christ. The words "he is risen; he is not here" activate our hearts, and we join in the Easter vigil liturgy to celebrate the newness of light, fire, water, exultation, and song. We are moved by the lilies in the field, the sunrise in the meadow, the updraft in our hearts.

Somewhere in our hearts, each morning, we experience an Easter moment. With a flood of resounding confidence, we see the world born anew—a world without poverty, without landmines or toxic water. We see a world we once thought of as inert come to life.

Ralph Metzer, an ecological philosopher in the San Francisco Bay Area, is a sage in the area of the dynamics of life, death, and rebirth. When I heard him speak with deep conviction about the connection between life and death, I better understood how the creative process is embedded in the dynamics of nature and soul. Continuing my reflection, I realized that what the culture calls "creativity" my tradition names "resurrection." Don't the scriptures say that at death, life is changed, not ended?

From this perspective, the world looks entirely different, and the commitment to heal the strife among culture, race, and creed takes on new meaning. Winter turns to spring, the crocus bursts into bloom, robins return, and the sun dispels the darkness. Once again, we see that the world holds out the promise of something entirely new; this evolutionary vision keeps hope alive. We trust that tomorrow can be different than today. We read with new understanding the scriptural words "he is risen; he is not here."

Easter reminds us that through the resurrection, life is changed. We begin anew to ponder the lessons of the empty tomb. Like Doubting Thomas of the scripture, we put our hands into the wounds of the Earth and pursue new life. We envision a new planetary culture being born in our midst. We become inspired by the projects of peace arising out of the resurrected souls of the people.

New friends, new music, new conversations, and new gatherings happen across the land. As people of the empty tomb, we can read about and reflect on the needs of the world, and identify organizations that further causes we wish to support. We can gather in living rooms and churches and community centers to share our experiences of a wounded world and to collectively enact a new Easter moment of hope and healing.

Cosmic Tendencies and Psychic Depths

The cosmos—with its dynamic principles of interconnectedness, diversity, and depth—presents to the landscape of human engagement a path we can walk toward: a world of harmony, balance, and peace.

Concomitantly, the human psyche, which is born into goodness at the depths of its being, is genetically coded for creativity and compassion. Properly disposed and activated by prayer and spiritual practice, we are challenged and empowered to translate into cultural form those tendencies that emerge from the deep recesses of the human soul and the dynamics of the universe.

In the language of geo-justice and engaged cosmology, I propose that humanity today live with a preferential option for the Earth. By that I mean, may we hold Earth high. As a planetary people, may we remember our origins. Drawing on the recesses of our psyche and the tendencies present in the culture and creation, may we move forward to celebrate the freedom, equality, and self-realization of all manifestations of gender, color, and class.

Today, in fact, I believe the human psyche has moved forward into another mode—a mode of engaged cosmology that reaches beyond geo-justice to embody the expression of harmony, balance, and peace. This mode is a vision that manifests when we become aware that love and holistic healing are at the center of all we hope and aspire to see realized.

As our inner depths are activated, we experience the call to give shape to new forms and patterns of human existence and culture. We become inspired to experience and express the beauty of the universe in personal, cultural, and planetary forms.

This vision and its manifestation will result in an integral whole—the culminating act of the human and the deepest realization of the universe and humanity's cosmic journey.

Creative Dialogue

I propose the creation of a dialogue between science and spirituality. We explore the challenge before us now. The challenge is to come up with a creative and imaginative response to the needs of our time, to fashion something entirely new. Our challenge is to be liberated from a fixed and finished universe, and to move toward a world that is vital, alive, and ever unfolding.

With Teilhard de Chardin, we envision a planetary community that transcends the straitjacket of the nation state. Teilhard writes, "The age of nations is past. The task before us now, if we would not perish, is to build the earth."

We are now able to envision a world that celebrates Earth, art, and spirit. In this way, we are able to make possible an integration between the observable dynamics present in the universe and the impact they have within the recesses of our soul, and ultimately on the planetary community, as well.

We envision a planetary community wherein creativity flows into every crevice and component. Meister Eckhart writes, "What does God do all day long? God gives birth.

From all eternity, God lies on a maternity bed giving birth." We ponder these words and realize that the divine is constantly creative, and that we are never more divine than when we ourselves are creative.

Stories: Channels for Creative Engagement

Thomas Berry composed his essay "The New Story," which he published in 1978, at a time when there was a strong sense of alienation in the culture. Existentialism and the death of God were dominant themes, along with a general lack of energy and enthusiasm for spiritual traditions. Thomas's universe story challenged the pervasive cultural and spiritual morass, and infused fresh energy into our personal stories, while creating a renewed appreciation for religious traditions.

Thomas helped us see that our personal stories and religious stories are paragraphs in the universe story. All our more personal stories are bound together in the compassionate embrace of one great story. These stories tell us where we've been and provide indications of where we are going. They activate our imagination and open channels of creativity, and become instruments of creativity, vision, and hope.

I have come to see my life as composed of stories that weave together tapestries of insight, wisdom, and purpose. Here I relate to you three stories—personal, religious, and cosmic— and then describe how putting these together opens the way to an engaged cosmology.

Personal Story

My sister, Mary, had for years been involved in researching the Conlon story. She would on occasion go to Utah to uncover information. When she learned that I was going to Ireland to lead retreats in the Dublin area, she wrote to a number of people whose names she had discovered in her research. One of the people responded, which led to something amazing. I was able to visit the farm where my ancestors lived before they migrated to Canada in 1844. I met fifteen cousins, none of whom I had known about before.

On that visit, I joined in the practice of Cemetery Sunday, which is a tradition among the Irish people. They hold the liturgy in a cemetery as a way to remember and pay homage to their ancestors.

I have many memories of that visit; perhaps the one that remains most vivid to me is a question posed by a third cousin as we prepared to leave the area. He asked, "How long since you've been home?" Even though I had never been in Ireland, this comment assured me that in a very real sense, Ireland has been and will continue to be my true ancestral home.

Religious Story

My introduction to Jesus began when, as the youngest child of Richard and Elizabeth, I ventured forth with the family to attend Sunday mass in the village where we lived. However, with the exception of the Sunday liturgy and the family rosary, which we prayed each evening, religious practice and education had little impact on me during those early years.

When I was thirteen, Fr. O'Rourke met me one Sunday and announced, rather out of the blue, "You will begin on the altar next Sunday." As an altar boy, I was closer to the priest and the altar; however, I still felt somewhat uninformed about my Christian heritage.

I was eighteen when my mother died of cancer. Suddenly the reality of my mortality thundered into awareness. Questions about life, death, and the afterlife took on greater meaning. The innocence of childhood was shattered. Big questions about who am I (identity), why am I here (purpose), and what happens now and beyond the grave (destiny) began to encroach upon my consciousness.

At that time, I was headed for a career in the chemical industry, but as a result of my inner searching, I also enrolled in religious studies classes. I began to understand for the first time the foundational underpinnings of religion. What might have seemed like a review to my classmates who had attended Catholic schools was for me a new initiation.

Later on in the seminary, I was provided with the foundation of my Catholic faith. I studied theology, scripture, and ethics. I was prepared, along with my classmates, to teach and proclaim our inherited tradition. The rest of the journey involved bringing the tenets of my tradition into the world, and internalizing what I had received so I could share it with others and inspire them.

Universe Story

The universe also has a story to tell. It is a sacred story that began 14 billion years ago with the flaring forth of a great burst of energy and heat. That "bang" gave birth to hydrogen, which then turned into helium. As this magnificent story continued, stars and galaxies were born. And in an amazing cosmic moment, planet Earth was formed.

Many living forms emerged, until the human appeared. Life became conscious of itself. This story continues, and our lives unfold. We take up the challenge to compose a new paragraph to continue this great story.

Making Connections

My journey has been one of making connections between what I learned from scripture and tradition and my understanding of its implications for the world today. I encourage you, too, to write your personal and religious stories, and strive to understand them in the context of the universe story.

The following are some questions that can guide you in this process:

How can I understand my personal journey and the story of my inherited tradition as an integral part of the story of the universe?

How can understanding the universe story heal the alienation that comes from isolation in our personal stories and disconnection from our tradition?

How can my tradition be more responsive to the broken stories of our current world?

Our understanding of these reflections sheds new light on how we understand revelation. In addition to the written revelation in the Bible, we understand revelation as an ongoing event that is also manifest in the sight, sound, smell, touch, and taste present in every expression of the universe. When we bathe ourselves in the experience of creation and understand the experience as divine communion, we become literate in the scripture of the universe. By reflecting on the three dynamic principles of the universe, along with our personal story and the story of our tradition, we find that the commandments of creation become a new source of guidance for a just and ethical life.

The new cosmic story connects us to the ongoing revelation of divine disclosure evolving in our midst. As we ponder our story and the story of creation unfolding in our midst, our world becomes functional once again. Healed of alienation and separation, we feel the fresh energy surging through our psyches and our souls. We awaken to a fresh sense of origins and destiny, and set out to take our place in the great unfolding, determined and energized to once again bring peace, justice, and beauty to the planet and our own lives.

The Urgency of Now

The words of Dr. Martin Luther King, Jr.—"the fierce urgency of now"—remind me of the civil rights movement, the campaign for voter rights, and equality among races in this country. President Barack Obama picked up a similar theme when he used the phrase in his campaigns for the presidency of the United States.

As I reflect on this phrase, I realize that the opposite of acting with urgency is procrastination. This clearly points to a failed strategy. If we want to accomplish our work and get things done, it is not effective to put things off.

Relevant to the matter of urgency is a healthy attitude toward death. We approach death not as a punishment, but as a reminder that we only have limited time to accomplish what we are here to do; namely, to act creatively and embrace our life's work. The vision expressed by Dr. King and President Obama is accomplished with great wisdom, and is ultimately a healthy attitude toward death. With this attitude, we are able to view the limitation of time as a motivation to live creatively with the time we have.

A few years ago, when Thomas Berry was just becoming

well known, he had a limited support system around him. I wrote to Thomas and offered to leave my position and put my time and energy into advancing his work.

After some months of considering my offer, Thomas replied. His response went something like this: "This is not a good time to accept your offer. I am in the terminal phase of my work and I need to focus on that in the time that I have left. It is not the right time to join me in this venture." He thanked me for the offer, but he felt an urgency to accomplish his creative work himself. In fact, many of his most important works—accomplished with the companionship of colleagues Mary Evelyn Tucker, John Grim, and Brian Swimme—were published in his later years, after the age of sixty-five. Among these were *The Dream of the Earth, The Universe Story, Evening Thoughts, The Great Work,* and *The Sacred Universe.*

When I, like many others, visited Thomas in the retirement home in Greensboro, NC, he talked about death with calm reflection. He said that when he died, he was not going anywhere. His small self would simply join the great self in one great and continuous journey to his God. He taught us that death is a state, not a location. He also demonstrated that when we realize that our time is limited, we can move forward to be creative, with a sense of urgency in the time that remains.

One lesson we can learn from great teachers, such as King, Obama, and Berry, is that it is never too late to make a fresh start. It is not too late to create ways to revitalize and protect our endangered world. We can let the limits of time be a catalyst that moves us to embrace life's great mystery. This mysterious journey itself will prompt us to do what we are here to do.

Questions to Ask Yourself

How do you express creativity in your life?

How do you hope to deepen and expand your creativity?

We can understand resurrection as another word for creativity. How do you see resurrection manifesting in and through Earth and its people?

What are the resurrection moments in your life?

What If

What if my words
revealed what is going on within,
vibrations of beauty,
landscapes of wonder?

What if my words
enveloped me in mystery,
talked to me about questions
I have yet to ask?

What if my words
announced what is happening?
Only then could I put my head down,
slumber off to sleep.

Our Call

Humanity is called
to embrace a fresh ethical sensitivity,
to keep our imagination vital,
to focus our creative energies,
to make possible
the great opportunities of our time—
a healthy planet,
the spontaneity of a child,
and the greening power of the planet
across fields, rivers, mountains and trees.
We sink deeply into mystery,
and arrive at a place
where we shiver in amazement
at the vast universe
unfolding before us.

A New Paragraph for Life

I know
that poverty must cease.
I know this through the brokenness
and conflict in my heart.

I know
that protest is my prophetic act
and that the world is longing
for a new soul,
a new healing moment.

I know
that when we awaken
to our origins
and become truly human,
we bring hope to the children
and to the Earth.
I feel called today
to bring the people together
to break bread
and tell the story.

I feel called today
to be a mystic in action,
aligned with the dynamics
of the universe.

I feel called today
to give my gift,

to listen to the heartbeat
of the broken world;
to heal the fragmentation
of people and planet.

I feel called today
to celebrate
the wonder of creation
and respond to sacredness
and challenges of life.

I feel called today
to participate
in the work of my time,
to fall in love,
to feel at home.

I feel called today
to be inflamed with enduring hope,
to be at one with the universe,
to be touched by God.

I feel called today
to compose
a new paragraph for life.

The Fifth Theme
Our Vision Realized

A profound metaphor for the new global civilization is found in the word *Pentecost*. Pentecost implies a powerful divine presence that includes and affects everyone. It involves an awareness of the power and presence that find expression in energy, movement, and life.

We visualize a time when water will be pure, the air clean, food nourishing and wholesome. Women will share roles of leadership equal to those of men; they will be classified by their talents, not their gender. All people will have equal opportunities for leadership. Every person and system will be honored and praised, as all lend their collective energies to a world of grace, goodness, and beauty.

As we reflect on our time here, I invite you to continue to look over your life to discover and articulate the connective tissue that can reveal patterns in your life. Perhaps by looking back and forward in this manner, you can venture forth with increased clarity about the world as it unfolds before us.

Together we dream that our hopes are realized and our vision never dies. We take up the challenge to engage in a fulfilling and meaningful life, a life that we are meant to live. In our sensitivity to the wounded world around us, we envision a new global civilization that is ours to create through transformation of the human spirit, which makes beauty possible. We venture forth, our lives infused with the creative energy of the universe. Aware of why we are here, we cross the threshold into a hope-filled interconnected world, with renewed pride in being human.

We reflect on John's Gospel as we explore and contemplate the way ahead: "I am the vine and you are the branches." We are more than we could ever have imagined.

The Good Book reminds us there is a time for every season under heaven. Now is the time when a new day is promised, when we can together take the "long walk to freedom" promised by Nelson Mandela and other prophets around the world.

I envision a global civilization in which alienation has been overcome and peace reigns supreme. It is a time when something new rises in our midst. It is a time to turn away from structures of privilege and oppression and give birth to a world that is transformed and entirely different.

We look to the future, energized by a profound hope that tomorrow can be much more than today. John Haught speaks of a "metaphysics of the future." By this we understand that the universe is an unfinished drama, and our vision is one more step in opening to and co-creating within its ever-evolving vastness.

From the Arab Spring and the occupy movement, life continues to move on. On this fresh spring day, the television is silent and the daily newspaper rests folded and off to my side. I look out the window at the clear blue sky and my heart pulsates with a new awareness. My spirit soars. Is this not the new moment of society and soul we've been waiting for, I ask?

Across the country and around the world I hear a resounding yes!

Connecting Spirituality and Science

One of my goals for this book is to demonstrate that the science of evolution can be understood as the basis of a vital, re-energized spirituality. As Brian Swimme writes, "After science has roamed about destroying traditional cosmologies through every continent, it is now beginning to be assimilated into a new cosmological wisdom." Now, as we finally reach the fifth theme, the vision we realize is both scientific and spiritual.

The future we see is a dynamic synthesis of the objectivity of science and the subjectivity of spirituality. These two wisdom sources are no longer at odds. Instead, we have a radically new orientation in which evolutionary science informs spirituality, at the same time that the sacred universe is understood through our spirituality.

The challenge before us is both personal and planetary. Our creative call is to reinvent our culture and our lives so we can respond in a healthy and effective manner to the needs of our world. I believe that the universe finds its spiritual expression in compassion. Within our inherited tradition, we must respond with compassion to the insights of the new science. We take this approach conscious of the traditional approach to our spirituality through scripture and philosophy.

Our own spirituality can be best understood when we discover the profoundly spiritual process that is the universe itself. What I envision is a planetary Pentecost in which we experience a bonding of each member of the Earth community with everything and everyone else. This unifying principle holds all things in an embrace that will move us toward a shared destiny, deep liberation, and personal fulfillment.

Just as the lion lies down with the lamb, peoples of all nations, colors, and creeds become friends, companions for the days ahead. Every child, elder, ocean, field, and tree feels re-vitalized for the work to be done. Loneliness is healed. Alien-ation is dissolved, friendship renewed, and peace reinvigorat-ed and restored.

Now is the time to be born again, and to heal what is bro-ken. It is time to renew the face of the Earth and welcome all that is emerging within and among us. The way ahead ap-pears now more beautiful than all the pasts, as the planetary Pentecost descends upon us.

Something wonderful happens when we see what we have waited for and anticipated actually comes to be. We experi-ence a healing moment when we know that gatherings are taking place across the land . In barrios and in high-rise apart-ments, in gated communities and teepees, people gather to tell stories of their peoples, stories of the land, gospel stories, indigenous narratives, and universe stories. Pentecostal stories weave together a tapestry of hope, compassion, and friend-ship to heal and make possible a world that is exactly what humanity needs.

The World as You Would Like It to Be

Suppose I ask you this question: How is your vision different from that of the dominant, consumer-driven culture?

Consider how your vision is different from the vision the media creates for us each day, with its abundance of advertise-ments about everything from Botox to Viagra, and its prom-ise of perpetual youth and vitality. More is better, we are told, and enough is never enough. The media holds out the illusion that true happiness will only result if we purchase the next new product. Linguistics scholar Norm Chomsky and oth-ers have characterized this as *manufactured consent*, in which the media creates a need and offers the solution through the products it promotes.

In the face of these deceptions and half truths, it is difficult to know what to do. One way I suggest to make possible the world we long for is to create a vision of the future that supports the well-being of the planet and is aligned with the beauty and wonder present in Earth itself.

With this approach in mind, the Earth becomes our mentor. Society is best understood as a network rather than a machine. When we embrace this consciousness, we are empowered to transform others, who in turn become participants in this newly fashioned interconnected world.

It is a world born out of a new religious sensitivity that will heal alienation, calm anxiety, reduce our affinity for the consumer world, celebrate beauty, and empower people to transform the tragic conditions of life. It is a world supported by a new wisdom that celebrates and embraces the best of sacred texts, honors our inherited traditions, and is awake to the ultimate mystery of the Earth and the cosmos. We look to the future with confidence and hope and see a world energized by a vision of mystery that will be realized and never die.

Vandana Shiva, scientist, author, and prophetic voice for Earth and its peoples, speaks out from the East. She calls for the end of oppressive structures that separate people from the planet, and the haves and the have-nots from each other. She challenges us to sow the seeds of love, protect the rights of nature, and always remember that we are connected. Through compassion and solidarity, we are invited to create a global vision of the web of life and move forward, aware that acquisition alone does not produce happiness. This vision resonates with the words of Mahatma Gandhi: "The world has enough for everyone's need, but not enough for everyone's greed."

Contemplation: Doorways to the
New Global Civilization

Answer these questions for yourself. Then, if possible, share your contemplation with some companions:

How do you name your spirituality?

Describe how your spirituality brings fulfillment to your life.

Write down your vision of the world you would like to create.

Describe how you envision contributing to a more healthy and just planetary community.

What lessons from your experiences of work, education, and relationships have influenced your present level of awareness of the world?

How do you see yourself predisposed at this moment to bring value and purpose into the world in a way that will result in personal fulfillment and deep cultural change?

Come Home to the Earth

As people called to unite the science of the cosmos and the theology of the soul, we take up practices that will deepen our awareness. We bring our attention to the God we cannot see, hear, touch, or smell, but who is fully available to us through everything we can experience. We take time to reflect on the gift we have been given as humans; that gift is conscious self-awareness.

You may find it helpful to reflect on the origin of the universe and the transformational events that followed the great flaring forth—the formation of the galaxies and stars, the beginnings of life, and the flourishing of the human with the gift of conscious self-awareness.

When we bathe in the beauty of creation and allow both the ghetto and the garden to touch our soul, we are being nourished. It is here that the universe and the psyche meet.

You may wish to read the works of medieval mystics Francis of Assisi, Hildegard of Bingen, Meister Eckhart, and John of the Cross, as well as become familiar with the writings of Thomas Berry and evolutionary philosopher Brian Swimme, and with the reflections of theologians John Haught and Ilia Delio.

You may also wish to spend some quiet moments reflecting on and deepening your awareness of the God of the cosmos, who has "come home to the Earth." Become aware that you are immersed in the divine presence every moment of your life.

Questions to Ask Yourself

Thomas Berry speaks of "the dream of the Earth"; what does this dream look like to you?

How would you like to be remembered?

What do you envision when you contemplate a planetary Pentecost being born in our midst?

How will you participate—with others in person, in cyberspace, or within your own heart—to move toward the planetary culture emerging out of the darkness at this defining moment in human/Earth history?

Machines No Longer

No longer do I live in a world of machines and separation.
No longer do I view my body as a cadaver
or separate from my mind and soul.
No longer do I see caged chickens
suffering in their incarceration
as simply maladaptive machines.
No longer do I see the world as I once did,
as the dominant culture prompts us to see it.

Today I have a new view of the cosmos.
I have a new way of understanding
how things emerged in the beginning
and the sequence of transformations that led to the present.
Even from the primordial flaring forth
there was a consciousness as well as the physical universe.

The universe I now see
has immense and wonderful powers
beyond any statistical measure.
My awareness has shifted from a world of machines,
a world lacking a sensitivity and soul,
to a new spiritual reality,
a new way of rooting ourselves in tradition
and becoming alive and present in the universe.

Welcome to a stirring in the culture and cosmos,
a new sense of place where everything belongs.

A New Tapestry

We move forward,
embrace the planet,
both beautiful and magnificent,
inspired by a vision that calls us
to heal, renew and resacralize the Earth.

As we listen deeply
to the promptings of the heart,
we experience the cosmic power
coursing through our lives,
calling us forward
into a life of courage, dedication and trust.

Like weavers of the past,
who created a beautiful fabric
out of diverse threads,
we see coming into awareness
the new tapestry
of a global civilization,
vital, strong, vibrant and forever new.

Our As Yet Unfinished Journey

I feel a joy of friendship,
gratitude for wisdom and gifts.

Recollections of hope, and appreciation for
friends met, challenges faced.

Embrace our unfinished universe,
each moment only a call to the future.

An invitation
to the not yet of our lives.

Bow to the possibility,
remember what is still possible to do.

Look back in gratitude,
look forward with trust.

Give thanks for a good companion.
We venture forth together.

Manifest your journey,
with the universe in mind.
So may it be.

Part III

Putting the Themes into Action

Chapter 1

Companions for the Way Ahead

Each of us can say that our life has been energized by colleagues, mentors, and friends who have supported us. Msgr. Jack Egan was one such person in my life.

I met Jack at Notre Dame University in the spring of 1971. He was on sabbatical from the Archdiocese of Chicago, after suffering a severe heart attack during his previous assignment. He had been invited by Notre Dame President Fr. Ted Hesberg to come to the university to recover and rest.

While at Notre Dame, Jack invited directors from social justice programs around the country to a gathering at the university. The focus of their meeting was to assess the important issues and explore how these programs could receive support from each other in dealing with their concerns.

Hundreds responded to Jack's invitation. Activists from many denominations, and also people struggling with urban issues as well as rural life problems, showed up. I was fortunate to be a participant in the early years of this venture. They called themselves Catholic Committee on Urban Ministry, or CCUM. Through the 1970s and well into the 1980s, the work continued. People who were at the edge of the church community but at the center of these issues became involved. CCUM grew to a membership of more than five thousand,

and religious leaders across the country caught a second wind. Mobilized through a newsletter, phone trees, a timely note from Jack, and annual gatherings, CCUM thrived. In many ways, these were the golden years of the movement.

The Gospel of Jack Egan

Jack spoke to me one day as I drove him to the Toronto Airport following his visit to support my work at the Toronto School of Theology (TST), where we had inaugurated a social ministry committee that was designed to provide field placements for TST students in programs of social justice.

As we approached the airport, Jack said, "Canada needs a Jack Egan!"

Those words inspired and altered the focus of my future work. I was deeply influenced by Jack's support and confidence in me. I loved his vision. It went something like this: "What people need is information, support, and the possibility of common action." I called it the gospel of Jack Egan.

Jack's vision was based on the conviction that we are not alone in our struggle, and that tomorrow can be different from today. The title of CCUM's newsletter, *Connector*, embodied Jack's vision and focus. He himself was a gifted connector with the ability to find something good in everyone, and the habit of reaching out to people on the fringes. He believed in the incarnation and had a deep faith in what people can do when they feel someone cares about them and will take care of them.

Jack and his colleagues repeatedly journeyed across the country and visited people and projects engaged in the work of justice, often in lonely and isolated places. Following one such visit, a person involved in the justice project stated, "I no longer feel separate from the roots of my tradition. I now know where to turn and receive the support and information I need for my work."

Jack also said, "Organization is the first act of justice making."

After our conversation on the way to the airport, I developed projects in Toronto and across Canada. I called the local group Catholics for Social Change and the national gathering The Institute of Christian Life in Canada. We published the proceedings and worked to build a network for justice across Canada.

Like each of us, projects and programs have a natural lifespan. They are born, grow and expand, and at some point they crest and inevitably decline. However, the visions that nourish such projects can hold continued life. Like land that is allowed to go fallow, they can be restored and bear abundant crops if given the chance once again.

Most recently, the vision that has propelled me over so many decades gave birth to the Empowerment Project. It is my hope that, like CCUM, the Empowerment Project may provide energy, focus, and support for those who are engaged in the universe story, the great work, and creation spirituality in our day. May it encourage, inform, and support those who dedicate their lives to make possible the mutually enhanced world about which Thomas Berry both wrote and dreamed.

The Creation of a Movement

The phone rang a couple of years ago. It was Sr. Kathy Thornton RSM calling from her home in Iowa. We had served on a committee on spirituality and justice with the Call to Action Program for Church Renewal some years before. When we met, Kathy was the executive director of NETWORK, a co-alition of women religious (nuns), based in Washington DC, that advocates with the US Congress for federal policies and laws promoting economic and social justice.

In our conversation, Kathy shared that she had followed my work since our last meeting and wanted to get back in touch to talk about our common interests. She indicated that she knew a growing number of people interested in the universe story, the great work, and creation spirituality. I invited her to visit the Sophia Center at Holy Names University so she could meet our faculty and students and see our work firsthand. I also told her about the Empowerment Project, which we had recently launched. We spoke about our common desire to create a series of gatherings for people who are interested in exploring how to take action in a manner consistent with their interest in creation spirituality and the new cosmology. Later, she sent me a list of books that she and her colleagues had been reading, and we added those books to the Empowerment Project's website.

As I continued to ponder my conversation with Kathy, a renewed energy infused my imagination. I saw that the five themes described in this book, along with the Empowerment Project itself, could serve as a guide for conversations springing up across the land. I was reminded of what Thomas Berry said when asked about the focus of his work: "I am here to build a constituency." In a similar way, I hope that the Empowerment Project can contribute to the creation of a movement that will bring peace to the planet and justice to the people.

As people gather to reflect on the five themes, I visualize good companions coming together in homes, churches, and community centers. May they, like Teilhard de Chardin, rediscover fire. May they enter the Ecozoic era of Thomas Berry, in which we live in a mutually enhancing relationship with the Earth. May they become participants in the blessed unrest of environmentalist and entrepreneur Paul Hawken, who inspires us to change our relationship with the Earth and ourselves so we can move "from a world created by privilege to a world created by community." May they respond proactively to the great turning of eco-philosopher and Buddhist teacher Joanna Macy, who teaches us to transform apathy into interconnectedness through what she terms The Work that Reconnects.

The Empowerment Project

The Empowerment Project marks the continuation of the work of creation spirituality, the universe story, and the great work that has been generated at Holy Names University (HNU) and other places around the world for more than three decades. I see it as a culminating act as we join together to give birth to a new global civilization. We draw on the wisdom of the prophets of yesterday and today, including Teilhard de Chardin, Thomas Berry, Mary Evelyn Tucker, Brian Swimme, and countless others,

There is a palpable presence among us. In every grain of sand and every human heart, there is a quickening, a forward movement, an anticipation, as a growing number of seekers experience what feels like a divine summons to venture forth to realize their collective destiny and respond to what is being asked of us. We can do together what we could never do alone. As people positioned at this defining moment in human/Earth history, we take up the challenge to make shareable this new initiative of transformative and innovative work.

The Empowerment Project brings together companions around the world who empower others with the ability to act, to reflect on their personal story and the story of their community, and to engage in the great work. The uniting vehicle is the website at www.empowermentproject.us. Although initially involving graduates from HNU, having an online presence allows like-minded people to connect from all corners of the globe. Companions join their energy with local and regional groups to respond to the unfolding universe and the needs of the Earth. Outcomes may include projects related to ecology, homelessness, hunger, health, or whatever the participants decide will best meet the needs of their community. I encourage you to visit the website and participate in any way that draws your interest.

Hello Maple and Pear

I go among the trees.
The tall maple in my backyard
is so green and orange,
golden and gorgeous,
in the fall.

And the pear tree,
stands stately
at the edge of the garden,
in the autumn sun.
Neither ripe
nor green,
just itself,
it offers its luscious gifts
to all who stop
and gaze upon the garden
just ahead.

Companions

"We will break bread together."
This phrase has a familiar ring.
It's all about companionship,
shared food, common vision
and great work.

Is it not an invitation to belong,
to participate in a common journey,
to embrace the mystery,
in this free and fierce world,
where there is always reason to hope?

The Dream Will Never Die

I honor and celebrate
the people who have gone before,
and all their programs.

I honor and celebrate
the friends of God and prophets
who have left behind
a legacy of love, wisdom and change.

In a society that is too eager
to surrender to what has gone before,
how do we challenge people
to decide what to do with their lives?

Society today is in search of wisdom,
and a guide who will move us
into the as-yet-unknown future.

The child in each of us
dreams about a tomorrow
that remains awake and alert,
that moves fearlessly forward.

Today again I ask,
What is my purpose,
what is my future?

It is about a dream and a hope
for a world filled with cosmic love,

a people and a planet
welcoming to everything and everyone.

It is about the experience of a life force
that permeates my whole being,
an overpowering reality that reveals
the connectedness with all.

Some call this the Great Spirit,
others call it God.
It is a power and energy I understand
as unconditional love.

My journey is best told
with curiosity and wonder.
In it, every new moment unfolds
to reveal yet another quest.

Chapter 2

The University of
the Universe

How can we translate the five themes into a language that speaks to the hearts and minds of people so they can alter our awareness and move us into action? I propose that through critical reflection on the five themes themselves, we will be able to change our awareness and move into a response that is what mystic and poet Richard Rudd calls involutionary as well as revolutionary.

Here, I borrow from the work of Paulo Freire, author of *Pedagogy of the Oppressed*, and Ursula King, scholar on the work of Teilhard de Chardin. Education provides a context wherein we discover our place in the universe. This is the original meaning of "university." Through critical reflection on our context, we take action to transform ourselves and the world.

Ursula King describes this educational process when she refers to Teilhard's writing in terms of a "zest for life" and reaffirms his message that each of us should live our lives with "great enthusiasm and energy." Teilhard's vision is complementary to our work, which aims to awaken us to the fullness of life, with all its joys and pains, growth, diminishments, and sufferings. Ursula also links the purpose and pedagogy of our approach to the work of Paulo Freire, saying that zest for life is "One of those 'generative themes' of which Brazilian educator Paulo Freire speaks: a theme that touches people so deeply that it can stir them into effective action for creating profound social change."

An Act of Liberation

Properly understood and experienced, education becomes an action of liberation. It begins with critical reflection upon the world. In our quest for personal and planetary freedom, we reflect on what holds us back. We discover who we are and become empowered to transform both ourselves and the world. It is about the discovery of context, science, culture, and personal story.

Education evokes in our imagination the vision and capacity to accomplish marvelous things. The educated person has the capacity to embrace mystery and become engaged in the transformation of the world. Education gives us a previously unimagined access to who we are and how we can serve. As the Italian physician, educator, and innovator Maria Montessori says, "Human consciousness comes into the world as a flaming ball of imagination."

We attempt—often within the constraints of an accredited university, but not necessarily—to step outside the huge cultural computer that programs our lives and to become in the true sense counter-cultural in a world of competition and consumerism.

We strive to reinvent learning. In our approach, we strive to oppose negative enculturation, conformity of any kind, and adaptation to an unjust system. We hope to become free from unjust patterns of thinking and living and instead embrace compassionate action. When the process works, we create new knowledge, not just repeat or pass on what is already known.

True education acknowledges that everyone is the true expert in his or her life and the issues and challenges that confront that person. In other words, each learner is uniquely able to understand his or her own challenges. The context, when properly developed, empowers learners to act on what they know.

Deep Learning

Education is a process, not a package. We strive not to become cynical or bureaucratic but to become sympathetic to both our and others' strengths and weaknesses as we move toward more compassionate engagement.

The educational process can be understood in the following ways:

Understand – Intellect
Experience – Imagination
Express – Heart and will

The primary sources for the educational process are the universe (cosmology) and our own heart (soul). At its best, education does not resemble an intellectual exercise that takes place in the realm of the hypothetical, with predetermined correct answers and conclusions. Rather, it involves genuine exploration and discovery, with a blurring of the traditional roles between teachers and students. Teachers also become students. Students also become teachers.

At the same time, learning and practice become one. In this praxis approach, learning does not exist just in a book; it also exists in the street and on the farm and anywhere there is a problem to be solved. In this manner, education moves beyond dualistic thinking and heals all separation. It represents a movement away from either/or and toward both/and.

Education is fully interdisciplinary; there are no isolated disciplines (e.g., psychology, science, theology). This approach dissolves the silo mentality of separate disciplines and instead focuses on collective wisdom. All involved in a learning community are challenged to demonstrate and experience respect, reverence, and responsibility. We are all students and teachers in the process.

Through our educational experience, we see the wisdom of Thomas Berry's words. We see our learning community as a communion of subjects, rather than seeing our classmates as a collection of objects. Our school is a place where wisdom is evoked.

Deep education is that which celebrates the vast expanse of the universe and the amazing emptiness in the recesses of the soul. Deep learning is about liberation and change. It is based on the conviction that we create knowledge through action. Our reflections on our actions move us into new ways of thinking, and from this new thinking, we begin to act differently. As this process continues, we move beyond any preconceived plans and are guided by a praxis approach. We remain open to the unexpected.

Deep learning is about how we live and think and are together as companions. It is a courageous adventure that requires risk taking. In the experience of deep learning, something dies and something is born. That is, we die to what we know and rise to new understandings.

Deep learning is both disruptive and creative. We often discover that conflict is the midwife of consciousness. In the process of truly learning, disruption is an indicator of insight and change.

Recognizing that people do not always initially recognize the value of deep learning for their lives, Freire focused on identification of what he called the *generative themes* that characterize a learner's world. He used codes, in the form of pictures and simple words, to draw awareness to themes that might otherwise be overlooked. For example, if the theme is oppression, the code could be a picture of an animal (e.g., cow, ox) with a yoke around its neck. To understand their experience of oppression, learners are presented with the code and guided through a series of questions:

What do you see?
What do you feel?
What do you know about this theme?
What have you done about it?
What do you need to do?
What more do you need to know?

Other themes could be ecological devastation, the need for a deeper spirituality, or whatever is generated from the group of people engaged in the process. Through this kind of deep learning, we are prompted to create actions that will transform the world.

Education as Life

Education is not a static exercise; it is a process that encourages and supports our participation and engagement in the world. We continue to learn as our lives and the culture evolve and unfold.

Education as not a preparation for life, but is life itself. We approach life as continuous learners. Graduation is not an end but another new beginning.

As we engage in the world, we continue to learn. Our cosmology and our enhanced consciousness prepare us to move forward. We move forward with the awareness that the dominant culture has a tendency to reduce people to things, to dehumanize them and reduce their dignity. We see each learner's life as a promise despite these forces of self-destruction.

Each learner's dignity and value are recognized. We view each person and ourselves as the subject of his or her own destiny. Each of us knows something and has experiences that are uniquely our own.

Each learner has a story with concerns, problems, and questions. Each has a deep desire for self-esteem and the feeling of empowerment as he or she moves forward to engage the world.

Each learner enters the educational experience with his or her own experience regarding issues such as race, class, gender, identity, pathology, and unique gifts. Each has his or her own challenges and expectations.

Properly understood, the classroom is a place where each learner discovers and experiences that he or she is worthwhile. Hopefully, the classroom reinforces the phrase "I am somebody," used by the Rainbow PUSH Coalition.

Each learner has a story accompanied by the experience of internal and external obstacles that holds that person back. Hopefully the educational experience will provide the opportunity to eradicate these indicators of oppression.

Vision into Action

Throughout history, great spiritual writers, such as Thomas Merton, have discovered that authentic spiritual experience inevitably leads to a life of concern and involvement in the social and ecological issues of the day. Some have named this process of moving from the interior world to outer action, from mystic to prophet, the "journey."

We can conclude that any quest for the experience of the living God cannot exclude the world in which the divine is fully present.

Over the years, movements in the Christian churches have pursued approaches to move our vision (spiritual experience) into action (prophetic work). The focus of this process is to dissolve injustice and to bring harmony, balance, and peace to the world.

To engage in a meaningful way and bring justice into the world requires us to see things as they are, not as we would want them to be. This requires that we remove any illusion or false consciousness about the world.

Critical Reflection

Through critical reflection, we are able to connect our vision to our action. We are able to name the world and our concerns through the metaphor of a tree:

- The roots of the tree are the economic system.
- The trunk is viewed as the political or planetary system.
- The branches are understood as the social organization.
- The leaves are seen as the beliefs and worldview of the people.

Through critical reflection, we are able to see how our worldview, including our spirituality, either supports or contradicts/critiques the status quo.

Our vision critiques injustice and the deprivation of beauty and well-being, and the impact of these on both the people and the planet. To move forward and bring justice to the world requires that the spheres of economics, politics, and culture come into alignment with our vision of the world.

Through our vision of a planetary community, we set out to take action to heal the pain of the people and the degradation of the planet, and to restore the fate of the Earth, both personal and planetary.

This is today's urgent and critical task, from which will flow the good news of the Earth that we are indeed called to be a prophetic people on the march.

Threefold Process for Participation

People take action to create a greater congruence between their vision and their experience of the world as they would like it to be.

You can participate in this process as follows:

1. View the world as it is (seeing)
2. Assess the state of the world from the perspective of your faith tradition and belief system (i.e., focus on the here-and-now situation in light of scripture and tradition)
3. Take action in response to an issue (i.e., a problem or concern you can do something about) and bring that action into alignment with your faith tradition

Through this threefold process, leaders will emerge and a movement will be born, as planetary people who with a common language and a common ground stand poised to embrace the headwinds of the future unfolding in our midst. As we take up the privileged task of creating a new global civilization, we acknowledge and celebrate the conviction that when people embrace and experience cosmic consciousness (the new story), they will be prompted to self-organize into cultural forms that celebrate diversity and interconnectedness, and to do so in such a way that the possibility of a new global civilization comes into focus.

We move forward into life, energized by a worldview that is sacred and empowering. With a sense of celebration, we transcend a static, disconnected world. Supported by the urgency of each precious moment, we courageously embrace each impulse to create the wonder and mystery of the new global civilization that awaits us.

Just for a Minute

There is a place,
a place of wonder,
a place that is holy, mysterious
and sometimes hidden.

A place I've longed for
all my life,
a place to visit,
embrace, plunge into.

A deep place
where as yet I have not been,
where I long to linger
to activate something
for which I have no word.

A place to discover and dream,
where just for a minute,
I know what purpose
and meaning can be.

Before Tomorrow Comes

Listen now
to the voice
of the hidden one,
that one over there,
in the back row,
almost unseen.

Listen now again.
Invite her
to the front row.
Together, let us sing and praise,
before tomorrow comes

Chapter 3
Thoughts on Going Forward

Our story begins with the origin of the universe fourteen billion years ago. Through observing the galaxies, Earth, and life itself, we discover how to enter emotionally and spiritually into our new understanding of the mystery and meaning of the story of the universe. As we engage in the great work that lies ahead, we both value our roots in the original flaring forth and also look to the future of Earth, art, and spirit.

Many of us experience deeply the desire to have more in our lives. Today, more and more of us are beginning to realize that the source of that desire is a hunger for God. Collectively, we realize that our lives are incomplete and we feel increasingly inclined to experience sacredness and depth. In summary, we could say we feel prompted to fall in love with life in the midst of the joys and sorrows that are the inevitable result of our sacred quest.

Each person's journey culminates in his or her unique quest for the living God. For some, their spirituality is marked by a discovery that "God is in all things and all things in God." Their experience of panentheism is expressed well by the poet Rilke, who writes, "It is spring again. The Earth is like a child that knows poems by heart."

Others search for the divine in the still, small voice of silence. The scientist Chet Raymo describes the spirituality of silence this way: "Catholicism remains even today deeply medieval—even pagan—in its rites, arts, and institutions.... The monastic cloister with its fixed round of prayer and rule of obedience to proper authority is the paradigm of Catholic faith."

As a cradle Catholic myself, I find Raymo's reflection to be true. I cherish the sacramentality of life that flows from the Catholic tradition. With the poets, I reflect on our lives as urban dwellers and ask, "Is there enough silence?" Often in Holy Week, I find myself searching for a place of silence—a hermitage, a retreat center, or aloneness at home—to listen to the voice we name as the Spirit speaking softly.

Silence gives us a clearer glimpse of who we are. John O'Donohue writes that silence is the victim of contemporary culture. Meister Eckhart says nothing in the world resembles God as much as silence does. Silence is truly the threshold of the spiritual life.

In our longing, we seek both solitude and interconnectedness. Silence may be the threshold, but love is the expression of its fullness. Trappist monk and member of Gethsemane Abbey in Kentucky, Thomas Merton, was walking to work with his publisher in Louisville one day when he had a mystical experience at the corner of Fourth and Walnut. He wrote that this experience was an "awakening from the dream of separateness." He felt that all sense of separation dissolved and he was able to love everybody. It is my hope that through meditating on the universe story, we can awaken to this experience of love and inclusion.

We can realize, as well, that what we seek was there all the time. We don't have to engage in a relentless pursuit. The divine is not an object to be prayed to; rather it is an enveloping presence, a subject to be felt, experienced, and embraced.

Our challenge is simply to realize that the divine is present in our midst and that we are deeply connected to the great web of life.

Make the World Better

Each era carries with it particular challenges and opportunities that are uniquely its own. Whatever visions and dreams we had for our journey, we know that when our time is up, we will leave this world and our work will be unfinished.

We live in an unfinished universe. There is still much that is possible for us to do.

In an unfinished universe, we move into the future without a plan, but with a vision. This vision may seem distant, yet it is realizable if we embrace the wisdom and possibility of a world shaped by reflecting upon the implications of Earth, art, and spirit.

Take up the personal and planetary challenge. "Make the world better," I hear a sacred impulse say. Be sensitive to the divine nudges that summon us to life.

Listen to the call. Listen deeply to the dream of a movement now close at hand. It is a dream for people of all ages.

Examine the world around you. Be attentive to the concerns that affect your life. View your concerns through the lens of your sacred texts and faith traditions.

Closing Thoughts

The work continues. We offer information, support, and the possibility of common action to people around the country and around the world. We envision a non-organization, or what we might call a self-organizing organism of inclusion, to make available the resources necessary to join this great adventure.

The goal is to replace the values of the dominant culture with a vision of inclusion and mutuality. This vision is founded on the conviction that when the new cosmology is properly taught and understood, participants will self-organize into social structures that are mutually supportive and congruent with their worldviews.

The approach I am suggesting is a healthy and healing process. It is about personal stories understood within the context of an unfinished evolutionary universe. It is an invitation, a personal calling, to participate in the future not yet realized.

We look to the future energized by the wisdom of our ancestors and the vision of good companions on the journey. We feel called to participate in the empowerment of people and the transformation of society and soul. We put our vision into action, dissolving the structures of oppression, liberating ourselves and others, and setting the captives free.

The future is ours to create as we imagine what our lives are about and what could possibly be in store for us. We realize that the only model for our lives going forward is the as-yet-unrealized potential of each person. Respect for each person's gifts of creativity and possibilities for fulfillment are central values throughout the process. The collective energy of the cosmological learning community contains a tremendous potential for cultural transformation and change.

The future that awaits us will draw on disciplines and practices from a wide spectrum of people, cultures, and regions. From the community organization approaches of Saul Alinsky, the liberating theology of Gustavo Gutierrez, the transpersonal vision of Dr. Stan Grof, the work of Carl Jung, the cosmological visions of Teilhard de Chardin and Thomas

Berry, and the contemplative wisdom of Thomas Merton and Thich Nhat Hahn, we see up ahead a world of harmony, balance, and peace. It is a world in which every creature and every member of the family of creation will fulfill its original purpose and collectively create a new global civilization that is a celebration of Earth, art and spirit.

The Way Ahead

Make possible a new global civilization.
Feel deeply the urgency of the moment.
Become seized by an impulse
to examine the current moment.
Make plans for the way ahead.

Move Forward

Move forward into action.
Heal what is broken.
Renew the face of the Earth.
Become involved.
Aspire to do great things.
Contribute to people's lives.
Embrace the reality
that you will leave the world unfinished
and your lives unfinished.
Become inspired.

Celebrate the work of Saul Alinsky.
Join a generation of seekers.
Embrace a passion of risk.
Remember and rejoice.
Times of vitality and influence
are times to celebrate.
Celebrate the legacy of your mentors and friends.
Celebrate the legacy of Jack Egan—
his vision of information, support and common
action.
Remain grateful for the times
when so many were touched by his work.
Recall with great thanks
the prophetic voice of Thomas Berry.
Within the new story,
the seeds of a cultural movement lie.
Celebrate the convergence of wisdom and vision
found in the writings of the medieval mystic.

Discover yourself in the universe,
as the universe discovers itself in you.
Become the planetary civilization
that awaits us.

We move forward,
energized by an awareness,
and sharing a common origin.
We are all cousin and kin.
In our interconnectedness,
all barriers are removed.
We become one people,
bound together
in a mystical prophetic movement
of justice, compassion and peace.

Flow of Thanks

O sacred one,
the place of blood,
where currents flow.

Standing on the shore
of my existence,
I watch and feel
the rivulets go by.

Quench each crevice,
I call,
follow the undulating language
of the heart.

You are here,
I cry,
muscle, sinew and more.

I am so happy now.
Let the wisdom flow
as I adorn the sacred one with thanks.

An Invitation

What can I say to a world torn asunder
by devastation, anxiety and unrest?
How can I offer solace and peace?

This is my invitation.

Ponder what it means to be human,
to create beyond war and violence
a community of healing and depth.
Envision a world of engagement and hope,
an awakening to identity and purpose.
Anticipate something entirely new,
a time of discovery of past, present and future.
Make possible a world of beauty in which
each human and other-than-human
can flourish and survive.

Be convinced tomorrow can be better than today.
Become a people of destiny,
agents of engagement.

Our journey toward a purifying sun
invites us forward into the possibility
of something entirely new.

Join the Becoming Planetary People community, watch videos with Jim Conlon (including a half-hour video that is a companion to this book and can be used for teaching and discussion), and find out the latest news at:

www.becomingplanetarypeople.com

Also by Jim Conlon

Sacred Butterflies: Poems, Prayers and Practices

Invisible Excursions: A Compass for the Journey

Beauty, Wonder and Belonging - A Book of Hours for the Monastery of the Cosmos

From the Stars to the Street: Engaged Wisdom for a Brokenhearted World

At the Edge of Our Longing: UnspokenHunger for Sacredness and Depth

The Sacred Impulse: A Planetary Spirituality of Heart and Fire

Ponderings from the Precipice: Soulwork for a New Millennium

Geo-Justice: A Preferential Option for the Earth

Lyrics for Re-Creation: Language for the Music of the Universe

Earth Story - Sacred Story